# A South Shields Education

*A short history of South Shields Schools. Not just facts and figures but mixed with memories of school days – some personal and many from others who enjoyed a South Shields Education.*

## Mary Shiells

*Acknowledgements:*

*WriteTogether & Members of the 'Family Story' Class.
Local History Librarians: Doris Johnson & Keith Bardwell, South Shields Central Library.
David Duffy & David Whale, Central Library, for advice and encouragement.
Shields Gazette for Photograph (p57) & cuttings.
Janis Blower for initial advertisement.
Contributors:
Alan & Peggy Atkinson; LilianDavison; RonDrew; Alan & Ken Drew; Graham Duncan; Muriel & Doug Hay; Joyce & John Erickson;Janet,Mandy&Graham Erickson; SheilaHenderson; Joan &Gordon Houlsby;AshleyWood; VeraKulkarni;WilliamT.Lugton;Frederick Parkin;Audrey Purvis; Doris Robson; Valerie Ross; Flora Rutt; Joan Steinson; Bill Thompson,(for advice); Mary Whale; Charles A.Willoughby for letters & early photographs.
Mrs L.Lilico, staff & children Westoe County Infants'.
Mr B.Winter, staff & children. Ridgeway JMI school.
      A sincere Thank You to one and all.
Books & References:
Ward's Directories 1895 to 1940
Kelly's Directories 1890, 1921, & 1925
Maps:1895, 1905, 1974 (Borough Engineer.So.Shields)
Segment A-Z 1988 (permission applied for)
The Borough of South Shields G.B.Hodgson
Centenary Book. South Shields. 1850 to 1950
Early History of Education in So.Shields up to 1930:
      G.Ernest Greenwell M.A.
Education Cuttings 1959-1970 (S.S.Reference Section)
S.S.Education Committee Minutes 1970-1997*


SHIELLS PUBLISHING. Tel. 0191 2654977
ISBN 0-9531971-1-5

## CONTENTS

| | |
|---|---|
| *Foreword: David Whale* | 4 |
| *I Find some Pieces of a Jigsaw* | 5 |
| *South Shields 1890* | 8 |
| *South Shields at the Turn of the Century* | 11 |
| *The First Decade    1900–1910* | 12 |
| *Maps 1894, 1905* | 14 |
| *The Second Decade    1910–1919* | 17 |
| *The Third Decade    1920–1929* | 22 |
| *The Fourth Decade    1930–1939* | 32 |
| *The Search for Jigsaw Pieces Continues* | 34 |
| *A Few More Questions Answered* | 37 |
| *Two New Schools 1936, 1938* | 42 |
| *The Fifth Decade    1940–1949* | 45 |
| *'Up the creek without a paddle'* | 46 |
| *Forties Continued* | 49 |
| *I Take a Walk    Monday 19.10.1998* | 56 |
| *The Sixth Decade 1950–1959* | 61 |
| *The Seventh Decade    1960–1969* | 70 |
| *Comprehensive Schools – The Debate* | |
| *Computers in Schools* | 72 |
| *A Personal View – Not Sour Grapes* | 75 |
| *The Eighth Decade    1970–1979* | 77 |
| *Maps: 1974 & 1988* | 80 |
| *The Ninth Decade    1980–1989* | 86 |
| *The Tenth Decade    1990–1999* | 87 |
| *Ridgeway School & children of the 90s* | 89 |
| *Westoe Infants' & children of the 90s* | 93 |

*ISBN 0-9531971-1-5*

## FOREWORD

*The author clearly demonstrates a deep interest in the roots of her 'South Shields Education', writing with enthusiasm of her search for clues, and the thrill of each small triumph as new information comes to light.*

*We hope that the library service may have played some small part in helping to piece together the jigsaw of facts and figures about the history and development of schools during this century.*

*Perhaps most fascinating of all are the many personal anecdotes from successive generations of Shields people. Readers will surely recognise many of the characters in the book, which in this brief account can only provide an intriguing and tantalising glimpse into our past.*

*It will be a fitting tribute if by stirring memories more material is forthcoming. History comes alive through stories about real people, and this book is most definitely about people.*

*David Whale & David Duffy*
*South Tyneside Libraries.   1999*

## I Find some Pieces of a Jigsaw    1998

Soon it will be the year 2000. It promises to be a time of celebration; a time to look back on the 20th century and for me, a time to put pen to paper.

I joined this century in 1930. I was born in South Shields, and lived there until 1953 before moving to Newcastle upon Tyne. When I was younger I went around with my eyes shut – civic affairs, organisation of them went over my head – that is until a South Shields group began to record their personal memories. I found their accounts fascinating, particularly when they wrote about 'School'... That was in 1992. At the same time I began to record my own memories and was dismayed at the gaps.

Almost by chance I discovered *Ward's Directory* in the library in its reference and local history section. I found I could put an exact date to half remembered things I'd been told as a child. I'd go to look up a street mentioned by my mother, Candlish Street as the place I was born, and found out the years they'd lived at that address and the year 1932, when we moved to Ashgrove Avenue, the home of my childhood. On each visit I'd search a little further and every tiny discovery was like finding a five pound note. I was able to trace where my Gt. Grandfather Corby lived; Taylor Street, that he was a trimmer in the mines and in 1900 he may have died for the tenancy changed to his wife's name.

One thing leads to another: not only had I stumbled on a way of putting dates to my own family history, I tried to find dates and photographs to back up my own school days but probably because of wartime restrictions, I couldn't find a single school photograph.

This interest in schools persisted. I began to make a few notes and rang around the family to check the names of half remembered teachers or lessons. Then I

asked 'Can you remember the school Mam went to?'
It was that question which made me realise, the few first hand facts I had were like a few pieces in a giant jigsaw. What is more, if I intended to search for answers about South Shields and its schools, then I should record them.

1897-1898     **Ward's Directory**     1897-1898

So. Eldon Street

30 Errington M. (Mrs)
28 Dinning J. rivetter
26 Wandless T. blacksmith
24 Mossman T. ins. agent
20 Palin S. (Mrs) dressmaker
18 Farrington J. T. driller
16 Corby J. fitter
14 Adams W. engineman
12 White M. donkeyman
10 Pickering J. painter
6 Darling A. (Mrs)
4 Lake J. J. teacher of music

1897-1898 p.190

**St. John's Terrace. G**

☞ Begins opposite Wellington ter
St. John's Presbyterian Church
St. John's Higher Grade School
1 Crane E. J. m. mariner
  Waugh W. clerk
2 Fletcher J. plumber
  Hunter R. ship carpenter
3 Metcalfe M. (Mrs)
4 Transom C. m. mariner
5 Hopper M. E. (Mrs)
  Rutherford J. customs
6 Smith A. gentleman
7 Wake W. cooper
8 Barker A. G. insurance supt
9 Hunter R. m. mariner
10 Woodall T. m. mariner
11 Norman P. clerk
12 Herring T. auctioneer
13 Lawson W. prov. agent
14 Wood W. sailmaker
15 Bushell J. B. house agent
16 Mouat M. (Mrs)
   Irvin J. (Mrs)
17 Atkin W. gentleman
   Atkin J. W. builder
   Atkin J. T. builder
18 Thompson F. & A. (Misses) seminary
☞ Ends at So. woodbine st

1897-1898 p.152

**H. S. Edwards Street. F**

☞ Bgns. at West Walpole st
3 Holman M. (Mrs)
5 Lalley M. caulker
7 Petrie S. shipwright
9 Simpson W. labourer
11 Boyack E. (Mrs)
13 Gudie J. mariner
15 Brown R. mariner
17 Marshall J. bricklayer
19 Banks H. plumber
21 Johnson J. H. blacksmith
23 Sherington M. mariner
25 Scott G. T. fitter
27 Bonhomme S. (Mrs)
29 Manson P. mariner
31 Abernethy J. joiner
33 Harrison M. miner
43 Flowerdew J. labourer
45 Maddison T. miner
47 Peacock J. mate
49 Wemyees A. mariner
51 Bell J. painter
55 Lowrie J.
61 Nicholson J. grocer
65 Alexanderson H. mariner
67 Dalton J. boilermaker
69 Downs W. painter
71 Parry T. painter
73 Carney P. driller
75 Lloyd J. shipwright
  Bennett E. grocer
☞ Ends at Bertram st
20 Miller G. N. grocer
18 Reid J. rigger
16 Knights G. furnaceman
10 Anderson B. mariner
8 Gibson J. mariner
6 Kerr W. caulker
4 Johnson T. fireman

**Taylor Street. F**

☞ Begins at Havelock st
7 McDonald J. irondresser.
9 Westerberg C. carpenter
11 Bradley J. W.
13 Nicholson J. fireman
95 Woods C. engineer
97 Corby W. trimmer
99 Beveridge A. (Mrs)
101 Ireland J. plater
103 Nodin M. (Mrs)
105 Ransom S. fitter
107 Bain G. joiner
109 King H. trimmer
111 Beck J. waterman

1913-1914

**Taylor Street. N**

☞ Begins at Havelock st
5 Harrison J. W. miner
7 Curry S. ironworker
9 Murphy J. donkeyman
11 Hyde H. stocktaker
13 Nicholson J. fireman
15 Potts J. rivetter
17 Crosby R. & A. gen. cartmen
19 Pass N. machinist
21 Craig T. rigger
27 Richardson F. waterman
29 Grundy J. Mrs
59 Crawford J. bricklayer
65 Sleeth J. T. miner
69 Redpath R. newsagent
73 Watson C. driller
77 Summerbell W. miner
79 Wilson T. rivetter
81 Heslop J. boatman
83 Ramsay T. S. blacksmith
85 Smith W. blacksmith
89 Davies R. boilersmith
91 Winship R.
93 Massingham J. postman
97 Corby D. Mrs
99 Cheyne M. mariner
103 Mitchison J. hawker
105 Ridley W. rivetter
107 Tait W. boilersmith
111 Peat R. rivetter
115 Wallace J.

**H. S. Edwards Street. N**
☞ Begins at Reken Dyke lane
Crosby R. & A. coal merchants
1 Blair R. fitter
3 Pollock C. Mrs
7 Harrison S. millwright
13 Cowen J. trimmer
17 Anderson J. foyboatman
19 Aikenhead M. Mrs
21 Georgeson J. mariner
25 Gibson T. shipwright
27 Pollard G. blacksmith
31 Peterkin J. G. rivetter
33 Biggs C. mariner
35 Goudie J. mariner
37 Jamieson H. B. fitter
41 Graham T. banksman
43 Fuggles W. mariner
47 Malone J. patternmaker
55 Neve M. Mrs
59 Marshall J. carpenter
61 Briscoe M. Mrs
63 McMorris J. Mrs
65 Erickson F. craneman
69 Lombard E. A. clothier
71 Burns W. engineman
73 Cheltenham J. mariner

1905-1906 p.142
**Coleridge Avenue. O**
☞ Begins at Readhead avenue
1 Swainston R. gentleman
3 Hopwood W. mate
5 McDonald J. clerk
42 Grey J. gentleman
40 McDermott M. Miss
38 Heron F. coachman
36 Fraser C. mar. engineer
34 Corby J. fitter
32 Robson J. coachman
30 Thompson T. mariner
28 Kell W. m. mariner

1928 p.188
**Candlish Street. J**
☞ Begins at Ladysmith st
1 Jennings J. builder
3 Williams D. miner
5 Thomas A. m. mariner
7 Wadham N. clerk
9 Grice V. R. m. mariner
11 Anderson A. mariner
13 Mansforth R. engineer
15 McCann C. ins. agent
17 Dale A. teemer
19 Patton J. joiner
21 Turner T. tugboatman
76 Ramsay R. m. mariner
74 Chapman A. trimmer
72 Brumby H. fitter
70 Johnson W. joiner
68 Corby J. fitter
66 Kinghorn M. P. foreman
64 Armsworth G. chief mate
62 Keen G. draughtsman
60 Hay T. plumber
Mica Lubricant Co. Ltd. works

1930 Candlish Street
80 Dunn E. policeman
78 Calder A. m. mariner
76 Crompton H. guard
74 Chapman A. trimmer
72 Atkinson R. m. mariner
70 Corby J. fitter
68 Thompson G. Mrs
66 Macdonald J. cartwright
64 Bertie W. boilersmith
60 Hay T. plumber

This idea for a small book took hold, but I didn't want it to be all facts and figures. I was more interested in the way personal memories brought the plain facts to life. Also my own friends and family could provide first hand accounts of school in the thirties and forties but what of the years before that time and afterwards!

I decided I wanted to start at the beginning. This was my century. I would start with 1900 and go on from there. I pictured a few pages of mainly facts, a basis on which my own schooling would make more sense – just an outline of the way South Shields schools evolved.

## South Shields in 1890    Kelly's Directory 1890

I found Ward's street lists full of interest but Kelly's 1890 felt brim full with fascinating facts and insights.

**Kelly's Directory 1890**

**So. Shields p.250**

SOUTH SHIELDS is a sea-port, municipal and parliamentary borough, market and union town, and by the Local Government Act, 1888, is now a county borough for certain purposes, in the Jarrow division of the county, east division of Chester ward, head of a petty sessional division and county court district, situated on the south bank of the river Tyne, at its confluence with the German Ocean, and at the north-eastern extremity of the county of Durham, in the rural deanery of Jarrow and archdeaconry and diocese of Durham, 20 miles north-north-east from Durham, 9 east from Newcastle, 7 north from Sunderland and 276 from London. On the opposite side of the river are North Shields and Tynemouth. The branch of the North Eastern railway from Newcastle has three stations, one at High Shields, one at Tyne Dock, and a third in Mile End road, within a few yards of King street, opened for traffic June 2nd, 1879 : there is also a branch at Tyne Dock, uniting South Shields and Sunderland, and the Marsden railway, the property of the Whitburn Coal Co. Limited, was opened for passenger traffic from Westoe Lane to Marsden in March, 1888.

South Shields was incorporated on the 3rd September, 1850, and is governed by a mayor, eight aldermen and twenty-four councillors, who also act as the Urban Sanitary Authority. The borough has a commission of the peace.

The borough (the municipal and parliamentary boundaries being co-extensive) is divided into four wards, viz. South Shields, Westoe, Laygate and Tyne Dock, returning six councillors in each ward.

The town, which extends about 3 miles from east to west, is populous and thriving; the streets in the modern part are wide, well lighted with gas and paved, but those in the older part, on the river side, are still narrow and inconvenient.

The town is well supplied with water by the Sunderland and South Shields Water Company, incorporated by Act of Parliament in 1852 : the supply is obtained from shafts at Humbledon Hill, Fulwell and Cleadon Hill, and is very pure. The Gas Works, in Coronation street and Oyston street, contain gasometers holding 1,900,000 feet of gas. The Gas Company supply Shields, Jarrow, Hebburn, Boldon and Whitburn, and have works at Jarrow as well as Shields.

South Shields (anciently written "Le Sheels") originated with the fishermen of the Tyne, who built here, along the southern shore, sheds, provincially termed "Sheelds," or "Shields," to defend themselves from the weather.

Fancy! Our North Sea was once called the German Ocean. Ocean Road of course! And Cleadon Hills, 'my' Cleadon Hills where in the thirties we trailed up Quarry Lane with a bottle of watery fizz and a few sandwiches for our picnic – supplied water to the town which was 'very pure'. I liked that.

Further on we read about 'paving, lighting, cleansing'. There is a clear outline of its salt works, of small docks then Tyne Dock, of warehouses and sidings, coal and coke, imports and exports. We learn of numerous railways and branch lines between the river side and coal mines. All this in 1890 and earlier!

In 1848 there was a separation from Newcastle upon Tyne and South Shields became a port in its own right. Here again the close packed facts come alight:

'The Custom House... opened 1864... a building in the Italian style... ' and this same near derelict building, in 1992/3, was refurbished and is now theatre, cinema, and art gallery with the River Tyne at its doorstep.

In 1890, we had a South Pier, begun in 1856, many churches (a study in itself), the Town Hall in the Market Place built in 1768, The Savings Bank, Barrington Street – this reminds me of school savings in 1936 and the importance of handing in the white savings book and 2/6d to the teacher. There was a Public Library and Museum in Ocean Road, the Ingham Infirmary on Westoe Lane (public subscription 1873), Public Baths and Wash-houses, Derby Street, The Fever Hospital (Deans), and two cemetries: Westoe and the newer Harton Cemetery. Again memory stirs: I remember childhood days of 'What shall we do?' and together with friends, making the long trek from home to Harton Cemetery, walking solemnly looking for the family grave, the name ERICKSON in capitals on the headstone. Families could purchase ground for four persons. Next to it was my cousin George, died at two years. No room for him in the family grave with his sister Jessie, four years, but we were comforted because his had a beautiful white angel under a dome of glass over him. Such ornaments were very usual in the thirties and stayed undisturbed for years. The wartime bomb, a direct hit, was a true vandal of many graves. The outline continues: salt, chemicals, glass. It speaks of the Market, the Volunteer Life Brigade, The Marine School 1868, founded by Dr.Winterbottom, its Principal, Ambrose T.Flagg MA and surely this links with Miss Flagg who left a fine legacy of South Shields photographs. Memory jumps too at the mention of the Marine Parks, Marsden Rocks, The Lawe, the Roman remains. Once, local history was of little interest to me, but now as this 20th century comes to a close, this outline of South Shields in the Kelly's Directory is not only exciting but reassuring. All that 'preparedness' long before I was born and the Town, and Cleadon Hills and Marsden Rock still there today.

**Kelly's Directory     1890    South Shields Schools**

P 257

Board schools accommodation, 7,985; voluntary schools accommodation, 3,644

Board Schools now in course of erection off Westoe lane, will provide additional accommodation for 2,003 children

BOARD SCHOOLS.

Cone street (mixed & infants), for 403 boys, 396 girls & 351 infants; average attendance, 399 boys, 282 girls & 331 infants; P. Murray, master; Miss Mary Evans, mistress; Miss E. Parsons, infants' mistress

Baring street (mixed & infants), for 358 boys, 358 girls & 347 infants; average attendance, 344 boys, 371 girls & 392 infants; William Brockbanks, master; Miss M. E. Appleby, mistress; Miss M. H. Crawford, infants' mistress

Laygate lane (mixed & infants), for 399 boys, 363 girls & 366 infants; average attendance, 440 boys, 430 girls & 473 infants; James Ashworth, master; Miss Jane Anderson, mistress; Miss Robena Mercer, infants' mistress

St. Mary's, Whitehead street, Tyne dock (boys), for 476 boys; average attendance, 450; A. E. Cowling, master

St. Mary's, Hudson street, Tyne dock (girls & infants), for 374 girls & 195 infants; average attendance, 336 girls & 191 infants; Miss Clara Bushell, mistress

St. Stephen's, Mile End road (junior mixed & infants), for 660 children; average attendance, 617; Mrs. Mary Blench, mistress

Ocean road (mixed & infants), for 456 boys, 473 boys & 437 infants; average attendance, 430 boys, 429 girls & 482 infants; Alexander Scott B.A. master; Mrs. E. Brockbanks, mistress; Miss Isabella Laws, infants' mistress

The Barnes (mixed & infants), for 354 boys, 396 girls & 394 infants; average attendance, 323 boys, 492 girls & 276 infants; Charles Hall, master; Miss Elizabeth Morris, mistress; Miss Lucy Fish, infants' mistress

*Green's Home Industrial School for 60 children; in connection with the Wellesley training ship, No.Shields. The High School (for boys) Public Day Trust Company Mowbray Road, built 1885 at a cost of £6,000.*

*South Shields Schools at the Turn of the Century*

I set out to look at *'Schools'* – before, during and after my time there. In my search for facts I came across the town's history and have included the bare bones of the story. It seemed a digression worth recording. The outline was followed by a list of existing schools in the town: Baring Street, Laygate Lane, Ocean Road, The Barnes, Holy Trinity Commercial Road, St John's, to name but a few – old schools all but such familiar names to South Shields people.
A small note caught my eye: 'Board Schools now in course of erection off Westoe Lane, will provide additional accommodation for 2,003 children.' 1890

At the back of my mind was the question:'Which school did Mam go to?' It was still unanswered.

This early list of schools raised other questions. The High School for 250 boys, Mowbray Road, 1885 was established by public enterprise. I wanted to learn when and where the High School for girls was established.
Cone Street school interested me. Unlike the familiar named schools, I'd never heard of Cone Street until it was graphically described in a memoir by a friend, Bob Spence. I came across it again in a random search of Ward's Directories. 'Cone Street, W.T.Lucas Master.' The name rang a bell.

Another question was important to me – I wanted to find out about Cleadon Park Infants'; when it was built, some of its history, and whether my very early memories of it were correct. The infant dept. was in a long wooden hut with steps into a small cloakroom opening into the 'baby' class. A long corridor & doll's house. I remember a hall & dais *but where was it?* Was the hall in the newer brick-built part of the school?

## The First Decade                      1900 – 1910

*Lily May: third row from the back, 2nd child from left*

1900 is a good place to start. My mother Lily May Corby was born in that year and 73 when she died in 1973. In the photograph, in her braided dress, she looks about seven years old: 1907? The two school photographs have no clues on the back although we used to pore over them as children. We must have been told which school but it has gone. I had one clue and that was Candlish Street. I spent many hours running my finger down *Ward's* street lists looking for: Corby. James Corby, Lily May's father lived 1910–1932 in Candlish St. I *needed* a previous address & made a long random search. At last I found it: Coleridge Ave. The nearest school to both addresses: *Westoe Road!*

Accession of George V & Queen Mary July 22nd 1910

More guesswork but at least we have a date. I *know* my uncle was towards the left in the front row but which uncle? Uncle Tony was born 1903 and Jim 1906. It is so frustrating not to remember something we once knew. I am pretty certain both photographs were taken at Westoe Schools but I don't *know!* Both uncles stressed the strictness of teachers: 'Dragons!'

I do have another story attributed to the first decade. It seems that there were rumours that Laygate Lane school was 'sinking' and the little girls going into school would count the rows of bricks to make sure it wasn't. Years later the mother told her son when he too started there. Such stories stick in a child's mind!

*South Shields 1894–1896*

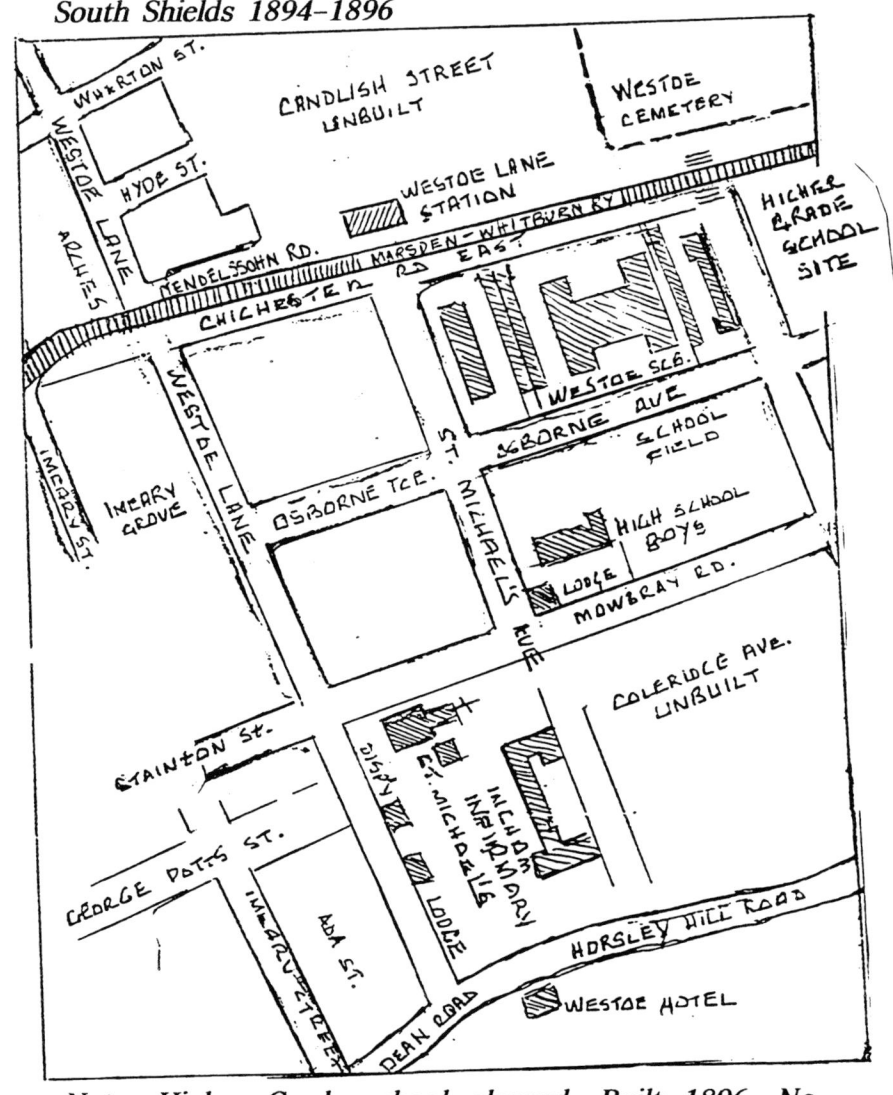

Note: Higher Grade school planned. Built 1896. No Iolanthe Terr. Westoe Lane! Streets around Candlish St.& Coleridge Ave. unbuilt until 1900–1910 .

*1905 street map of the Borough of South Shields*

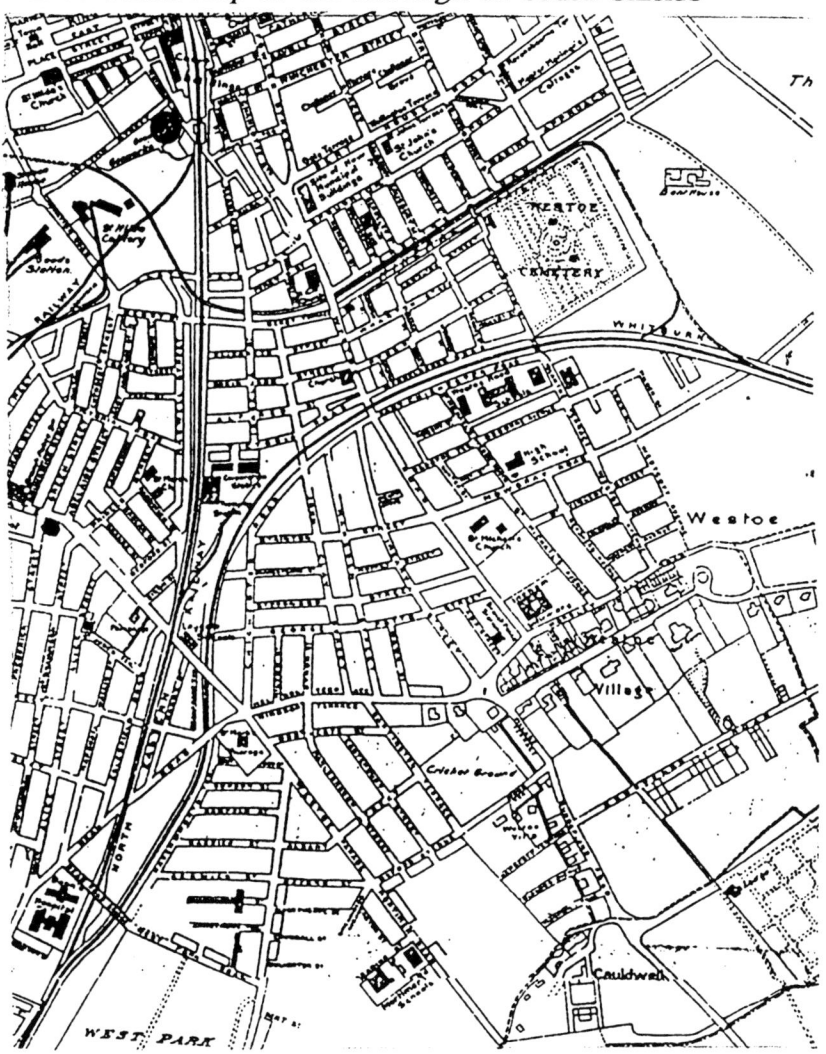

Coleridge & Candlish St. areas now built up. H.G. school 1896 now built on Iolanthe Terr. Site on Westoe Road for new Town Hall. St John's & Mortimer Rd. schools.

## Education: Changes and Progress

I remember the 'School Board' man! Even in the thirties he was a figure of authority. Really he was a left over figure from a time when teachers were paid by results. The South Shields School Board came about after the 1870 Act. Voluntary Schools became Board Schools but there were no great changes. Payment by results still operated throughout the country. In 1890, Kelly's lists of schools all show actual attendance figures.

It is to the credit of the town that elementary educ. kept pace with national levels. In 1903, South Shields Education Committee was formed: Board Schools became Public Elementary schools, new schools were built, and not forgetting the many church schools.

With elementary education well established, there was a demand by the townspeople for higher education. In 1885 a High School for Boys was built in Mowbray Rd. on Public School lines and backed by a group of private individuals. As a commercial venture, it failed and in 1908 it was taken over by the Local Educ. Authority. The Board built Stanhope Road School 1894, Mortimer Road in 1896 (enlarged in 1901).

After 1867, nationally, extra subjects 'Specifics', were required. In South Shields, Ocean Road offered Science/Art. Grant Earning & scholarships began to replace payment by results. Westoe Road Schools followed suit and offered science subjects.

If you know where to look, finding out a simple fact is easy *but* I'd often wondered *when* my old school, The Girls' High School was built. After some confusion I realised that the Westoe Higher Grade School, (see 1895 S/S map) built on Iolanthe Terrace, was my old school. It was built to accommodate the extra subjects then required. This Higher Grade School 1896 changed status when the 1902 Educ. Act designated it as a Secondary Day School. One more question answered!

## The Second Decade        *1910 - 1919*

I always felt that my mother, Lily May Corby by birth, was well educated. She liked words and knew her dictionary inside out. No matter which word we asked her to spell or explain, she never failed us. Although there were Higher Grade Schools evolving (from 1896) I still feel she was a child of the elementary system. She would finish school at age fourteen in 1914.
Westoe Schools developed as a grant-earning Higher Grade School offering Science and Literary subjects. I feel that if a scholarship were available to her we would have been told. Also, it was accepted then, that educational opportunity should be given to 'boys'. A clue to this convention must be the example of the High School for Boys, Mowbray Road. It was established in 1885 as a commercial concern by enterprising townspeople. Attitudes *were* changing but a further setback would be the onset of war in 1914.
World War 1 overshadowed the rest of the decade and South Shields schools showed little change over those years.
One change should be mentioned: a new Town Hall. The Town Hall, in Westoe Road, was opened in 1910: the total cost of buildings, £70,000. On the forecourt, a bronze statue of Queen Victoria, erected by public subscription. (no mention of her hand maidens)
Westoe *Lane* (1895 Ordnance Map) was now Westoe *Road* and the address for the Education Dept. was: Town Hall, Westoe Road.

I came to a stop at this point - no stories, no photographs. Even the *Pears Cyclopaedia* let me down.
I returned to my search & found a fresh lead. Under *Academies & Schools* in *Ward's* I traced the history of schools in the early part of this century. But best of all, I came across a photograph of my old school!

| 1903-1904 | 1907-1908 | 1913-1914 p280 |
|---|---|---|
| Baring Street (W.J,Weston) | Baring Street (A.M.Cubey) | **Academies and Schools.** Council Schools.—Baring st. W.J. Weston, master; Miss E. W. Reid, mstrss; Miss P. Richardson (juniors) mistress; Miss A. M. Cubey (infants) mistress. Barnes, C. Smith, master; Miss L. H. Söhns, mistress; Miss A. Tully (infants) mistress. Cone st. R. W. Brown, master; Miss M. E. Blakey, mistress; Miss E. Parsons (infants) mistress. Dean rd. J. Willis, master; Miss E. J. Winter, mistress. East Jarrow, J. Gillhespy, master. Gilbert st. Miss A. Tulloch (infants) mistress. Laygate, W. Smith, master; Miss M. A. Lincoln, mistress; Miss A. M. Vernon (infants) mistress. Ocean rd. J.W. Burcham, mstr; Miss M. D. Lang, mistress; Miss M. Robson (junior) mistress; Miss M.E. Hoare (infants) mistress. High School, Mowbray rd. G. R. Kirwan, M.A. master. Westoe (secondary), T. A. Lawrenson, M.A. master; P. Murray (senior) master; J. West (boys) master; Miss E. Morris (girls) mstrss; Miss Crawford (infants) mistress. St. Stephen's, W.Thomas, master; Miss C. Stewart, mistress. Stanhope rd. F.W. Marsh, mstr; Miss M. E. Appleby, mistress; E.Donkin (junr.boys) mstr; Miss E. Barker (junior girls) mstrs; Miss M. Peacock (infants) mistress. Mortimer rd. J. Wonders (senior) master; J.Robertson (junior) master; Miss R. Mercer (infants) mistress. St. John's, St. John's ter. and Winchester st. R. Davidson, master. Voluntary Schools— West Harton C.E. H. J. Hook, master; Miss M. Craigie, mistress; Miss A. S. Moss (infants) mistress. Holy Trinity C. E. Commercial rd. J. G. Finlayson, master; Miss C. J. Westgate (girls) mistress; Miss G. H. Cook (infants) mistress. St. Bede's R.C. Victoria rd. J. Walsh (boys) master; Miss M. A. Brady (girls) mistress; |
| The Barnes (A.Tulloch) | The Barnes (W.Smith) | |
| Cone Street (M.E.Blakey) | Cone Street (E.Parsons) | |
| East Jarrow (T.Stephenson) | East Jarrow Gilbert Street | |
| Laygate Lane (W.Brockbanks) | Laygate Lane (F.W.Marsh) | |
| Ocean Road (Jos.Willis) | Ocean Road (M.D.Lang) | |
| Westoe Road (Higher Grade) (A.Scott) | Westoe Road (SecondaryGrade) (F.Betteridge) | |
| St.Stephen's (W.Thomas) | St.Stephen's (W.Thomas) | |
| StanhopeRoad (M.Peacock) | StanhopeRoad (M.E.Appleby) | |
| MortimerRoad (J.Wonders) | MortimerRoad (R,Mercer) | |
| Green'sHome IndustrialSc. | VoluntarySchools: Harton Natnl. | |
| HartonNatnl. | HolyTrinityComm. | |
| Holy TrinityCh. | St.Bede'sCath. | |
| Marine School | St.Hilda's | |
| So.ShieldsHigh SchoolCompany. | St.John'sHigherGr. St.Mark's | |
| St.Bede'sCatholic | St.Mary's | |
| St.Hilda's | Sts.Peter&Paul | |
| St.John'sHigherG. | St.Simon'sNat. | |
| St.Mark's | GreenWinchesterSt. | |
| StsPeter&Paul | Green'sIndust.Home | |
| St.Simon'sNatnl. | Marine School SouthShieldsHigh School Co.Ltd. | |

*Schools: A Solid Foundation*

*Method:* First I had to *find* the Lists, photocopy, then take them home for closer study. On the bus I'd take a quick look. The lists at this point were before my time but the Schools were familiar and names began to jump out at me. Later when I came across: Miss A Henderson, it confirmed a memory for me and I was delighted. I began cross checking from one year to the next. I could see when new schools entered the lists: 1908 No Dean Road School. 1913/4 Dean Rd. J.Willis master; Miss E.J.Winter m'tress. I checked back and found J.Willis at Ocean Rd. in 1903. In a way these are names without faces but to me as I tracked their moves from school to school they became people again. Other patterns emerged: 1890 lists recorded actual attendance figures in line with 'payment by results'. By 1903 changes in the titles of schools reflected the move to Higher Grade/Secondary schooling. Some Scs. became Grant Earning & in this, South Shields kept abreast with national progress.
At this point I bought a book which had been recommended to me: *G.B.Hodgson's - The Borough of South Shields*. I turned to 'Education'. His fine account was confirmed by facts in the Directories: the book is an important historical record in itself.
In his book I came across a name: W.Brockbanks, master 1868 in a newly built British School in Hudson St. (p417) I checked the 1905 map for Hudson St. & found a tiny school near Boldon Lane. In *Ward's* list 1903/4 I found: Laygate Lane, W.Brockbanks, master. A much bigger school! Promotion?
It pleases me to find this connection between 'my' century and Hodgson's 19th Century. This feeling of continuity is reassuring. I noticed another small link: Ron Drew writes of Baring St. Miss A.M.Cubey(1927) & there she is in 1907. Another piece in the jigsaw.

## The Boys High School, Mowbray Road

*A fairly recent photograph taken by C.A. Willoughby of his old school.*

The High School, Mowbray Road, established by the Public Day School Company: built 1885. cost £6,000.

It became the property of South Shields Education Authority in 1908 at a cost of £8,562.

When the boys removed to the new High School at Harton in 1937, the building later became an annexe to the Girls' Grammar-Technical School, then used for Teacher Training, then there were plans for a hospice but the building was vandalised and later demolished, 'about four years ago in 1994.' Thanks to C.A. Willoughby we have the above photograph.

*Westoe Secondary School, Iolanthe Terr. in 1912.*

*Built as a Higher Grade School in 1896 under the Board School system: it was designated as a Secondary Day School in 1903 when it became part of the Elementary system. In 1937 it became The High School for Girls. In the late 80s this fine old school was demolished.*

A while ago I learned that my old school on Iolanthe Terr. had gone. It's the old story: a sense of loss when it's too late – and not a single school photograph!
Some years later I began to collect facts for 'Schools'. I'd covered the first decade, but 1910–1919 was a problem – no photographs or stories – nothing. On request, the local history librarian looked out half a dozen early photos. There it was, my old school: the side gate, the narrow yard, the high windows. In 1941 I'd entered its portals, an anxious 11 year old. Finding the photo felt special. I thanked the librarian warmly.

*The Third Decade*                        *1920–1929*
*A letter from C.A.Willoughby*
'Dear Mrs Shiells,
I receive the *Cookson Country* pages from the *Shields Gazette* each week from my brother who still lives in South Shields & notice that you are going to compile a record of local schools with photographs... please send me any information about your project...'
When I received the letter I felt I had struck gold. I could still confirm dates and changes from *Ward's* or *Kelly's* directories but here was a bright memory to flesh out the facts, so to speak.
I've already mentioned how names would jump out of the lists. One name in particular caught my interest: W.T.Lucas M.A. I'd made a note eons ago it seems: Cone Street, W.T.Lucas, master.
I'd jotted it down because Bob Spence had spoken of Cone St. & Mr Lucas was not just Head at the boys' High School, Harton, when Miss Dogherty was my Head at the girls' High School, Iolanthe Terr., he was also the father of a pen-friend I had, back in 1946.
It was just a coincidence on paper but it caught my interest. In an exchange of letters with my *new* 'pen-friend' C.A.Willoughby, I learned that Mr Lucas had been his Head & he promised to describe him for me.
C.A.Willoughby proved to have clear ideas. 'I'll talk about the Infants' Dept. first, then the 'Big Boys' and finally the High School where 'Bill' Lucas ruled supreme.' I enjoyed his letters, and very generously he gave me permission to use what I needed.
'I can well remember the happy days I spent as a child in South Shields. I started off in Laygate Lane in the early twenties. We lived in Dacre St. and then in West Park Rd. I then progressed to the High School, Mowbray Rd. I did take photographs of the High School some while ago but alas it is all boarded up and looks most derelict. Laygate Lane School had vanished

altogether... I see that Ocean Rd. School has vanished now – Asda rules in its place!' (29th July 1998) I leave Laygate Lane at this point. I still had some questions of my own. If there was a High School for boys as from 1885/1908 then what provision was there for girls? I'd heard of Westoe Central but I wasn't clear how it fitted into the school system. I turned to *Ward's* lists 1920p267; no mention of Westoe Central!

**1920.**

**Academies and Schools.**
Ainsley's Navigation School, Mill dam
Council Schools.—Baring st. W.J. Weston, master; Miss M. Tait, mistress; Miss P. Richardson (juniors) mistress; Miss A. M. Cubey (infants) mistress. Barnes,C.W. Smith,mstr; Miss L. H. Söhns (girls) mistress; Miss A. Tully (infants) mistress. Cone st. J. Gillhespy, master; Miss M. E. Blakey, mistress; Miss E. Parsons (infants) mistress. Dean rd. J. Willis, master; Miss E. J. Winter, mistress. East Jarrow, R. Cunningham, mstr. Gilbert st. Miss A. Tulloch, (infants) mistress. Laygate, J. W. Burcham, master; Miss M. A. Lincoln, mistress; Miss E. M. Dennis (infants) mistress. Ocean rd. R. W. Brown, mstr; Miss M. D. Lang, mistress; Miss M. Robson (junior) mistress; Miss M.E. Hoare (infants) mistress. High School, Mowbray rd. T.A. Lucas, M.A. acting master. Westoe(secondary), T. A. Lawrenson, M.A. master; J. West (boys) master; Miss E. Morris (girls) mstrss; Miss Johnson (infants) mistress. St. Stephen's, W.Thomas, master; Miss C. Stewart, mistress. Stanhope rd. F.W.Marsh, mstr: Miss J. W. Reah, mistress; E.Donkin (junr.boys) mstr; Miss E. Barker (junior girls) mstrs; Miss M. Peacock (infants) mistress. Mortimer rd. J. Wonders(senior) master; J.Robertson (junior) master; Miss I. Sutton (infants) mistress. St. John's, St. John's ter. and Winchester st. R. Davidson, master. Mowbray Infants, Miss Crawford, mistress.

Voluntary Schools—West Harton C.E. H. J. Hook, master; Miss D. E. H. Smith, mistress; Miss A. S. Moss (infants) mistress. Holy Trinity C. E. Commercial rd. J. G. Finlayson, master; Miss C. J. Westgate (girls) mistress; Miss G. H. Cook (infants) mistress. St. Bede's R.C. Victoria rd. Mrs. E. M. Stothard (girls)mistress; Miss R. Brady (infants) mistress. St. Bede's R.C. Boys', Derby ter. F. Walsh, master. St. Hilda's C.E. Coronation st. J. W. Parker, master; Miss E. R. Guest (infants) mistress. St. Mark's C.E. Hardwick st. Miss A. W. Judson, mistress. St. Mary's C.E. Whitehead st. J. Grayson, master. Sts. Peter & Paul R.C. Belle Vue cres. Miss M. Caulfield, mistress. Simonside C.E. Simonside, Miss E. E. Everson, mistress. V. C. Carter, secretary to the Education Committee, Town hall, Westoe rd

Davies J. E. Bridge chambers, 33 King st. See advt. page 8
Green J. O. & A. K. Misses, 10 Winchester st
Green's Home Industrial School, Mile End rd. (T. 641); B. S. Jones, deputy supt; Mrs. Jones, matron
Lee J..E. Miss, 6 Meldon ter
Marine School, 13 Ocean rd. (T. 486); H. R. Cullen, principal
Nautical School of Cookery, Mill dam
Robertson J. S. G. Miss, 224 Westoe rd
Stewart Misses, Westoe village

*Laygate Lane 1920s*    *Courtesy of C.A. Willoughby*

'Brother Harold, b.4.12.1916–May1941, war casualty- is 4th from the left second row from bottom. Possibly about ten years old. Miss Brown is the class teacher on the left & Mr Gillespie the Headmaster on the right. He retired while I was there & received an armchair as a present. Harold is sitting next to his friend (Tennant on the right).'

'I do remember Miss Dick... kind, wore spectacles and seemed to be partial to black dresses. Miss Hindmarsh a very large lady with her hair tied tightly back in a large bun, always surrounded by odds and ends of wool... we were always creating masterpieces from bits and pieces – long before Damien Hirst! I recollect open coal fires in winter. By and large we had a happy existence and the teachers taught us well.'

*Laygate Lane 1920s     Courtesy of C.A. Willoughby*

'Brother Arthur, b.22.11.1920, Deceased – 2nd from the left, 2nd row from the bottom. I think this was at Laygate Lane.' (Brother Reg, b.1931 went to Mortimer Road but spent some time evacuated to the Lake District.)

C.A.Willoughby's third letter covered his junior school years in the late 20s. He mentioned a Miss Laverick – 'On reflection... In those days teachers were unmarried or widowed. Married ladies were not allowed to teach. Miss L. was really a glamorous blonde. Sad to say she got married when I was there and had to leave, a sad loss to the young gentlemen.'

'My first teacher in the 'Big boys' was Mrs Smith, I wonder now, had she lost her husband in the first world war? A good teacher but feared by all...

Snowballing: Mrs Smith in the school entrance was hit in the face... one of those moments in a film when all motion stops and the sound is cut. The shouting came to a stop, a deathly hush... But great teacher that she was, she wiped the snow from her face and continued on her way, with dignity. The board was always filled with words; at home time the board was placed on the easel and Mrs Smith conducted with her cane the interlude known as 'spelling'. We all learned to spell quite efficiently.'

'I recollect a Miss Brown and a Mr Whyle. He was a rather dapper man with a small moustache, smart in his dress and wore spats on his shoes. He used to walk up the aisle between the desks and crack people around the head as he progressed... "What did our Lord Jesus teach, boy?" No reply. "Love boy, love." crack... There was Mr Bruce, probably ex-army, – in the yard the whistle was blown, once to stop in your tracks, twice to fall into line – Mr.B used to treat it like a parade – no talking in the ranks. There was a Mr Kelly who walked with a stick, again probably a war-wound – he was a very fine water colourist...'

Although my request for school memories brought in but one reply; Charles Willoughby's weekly letter was both fluent and useful. I wrote and phoned friends to ask their parents for first-hand memories of school in these very early years. I had the school lists in front of me and they showed the heads of schools, but what about the many, many teachers. I asked for memories, not libellous, for I had a wish to record just a few of the teachers as living and breathing people.

Val Ross replied for her mother: born in 1919, she went to Barnes Road then Dean Road schools. At Dean Road there was Miss Kay, a lovely teacher who died only recently; also a Nelly Dye, pupil teacher, who was a marvellous embroiderer, still living in South Shields.

My sister contacted a friend, Audrey Purvis by birth, whose mother had known Uncle Jim (p.12/3) I had high hopes that she could confirm Westoe Schools as the school my mother Lily May and her brothers went to. A.P.was in America. When she returned, she told my sister that her mother had died eight months earlier but she did have an early school picture of her mother at Mortimer Road' – *and,* she did go to Westoe School!

Perhaps I could make a mention here of Bob Spence, a fine writer, who died in 1995. He may have exaggerated just a bit but his work was full of life.
1927 'At the age of four I was taken along to Cone Street School... For those who don't know Cone Street – it was near the river between Taylor's Foundry and the Middle Docks. The ash from the foundry spilled over into the school yard. Those of us with shoes played on this at playtime. The windows had to be kept shut to keep out the foundry fumes and reduce the noise of the riveters' hammers.
The headmistress and teachers were strict but it wasn't too bad. We used slates & slate pencils, bead frames & plasticine... Four times a day the journey to & from school was under a dark railway tunnel. Usually I ran through imagining all sorts of demons lurking in the shadows... We moved house... At Mortimer Rd.School, as the sign outside said 'mixed infants' I became a mixed infant.'
Janis Blower's *Aall T'githor Like the Folk o' Shields,* Vol.2 shows Cone Street bridge and I thought of Bob.
     At this point I rang Ron Drew. He and Bob were both members of our Family Story group in 1993. I knew Ron had an early school photograph. Sure enough, he was able to put his hands straight on the original and he posted it to me the next day!
These early photographs are valuable. I have them copied locally & I am careful to return them promptly.

*Baring Street 1929*      *Courtesy of R.H.Drew*

*Ron Drew: 6 approaching 7, back row, end right and wearing 'the' sailor suit.*

'In answer to your question: My mother's Aunt was the head of Baring St. Infants. Miss Cubey, was of the typical Victorian mould and was extremely strict: but that did not deter her from giving me special privileges causing me much embarrassment! An example of this is referred to in "My Way" '

'I even started off school on the wrong foot. In my first week at Baring Street the Headmistress picked on *me* to sort the chalks into different boxes according to their colours. I thought this was great. I was the 'bestest' in the class. To the other kids, however, I was the teacher's pet... It was later that I found out that the Headmistress was my mother's Aunt Cubey... Imagine being sent to school dressed in a sailor's suit the day of the school photo! Not a day to remember.'

I remembered another comment in Ron's memoir: 'I progressed to Baring Street Junior Boys School... Mother had instructed me well. But it didn't stop me getting the cane and wearing the dunce's cap in the corner of the classroom.' I rang & asked, 'Did you really wear a dunce's cap?' I thought I'd discovered a real Beano/Dandy type dunce's cap! He replied that he couldn't say, hand on heart, that he had!

'When I was eleven I passed to go to the High School: later to be known as the South Shields Boys Grammar School.'

This short comment of Ron's also caught my interest. I return in thought to the school lists. Every time there was an education review: 1870 Act, 1902 Act, 1921 & 1944; there was a change in the titles of schools and systems.These changes make it very difficult to give a clear history of schools from the beginning of the century. A Higher Grade School built 1896 became a Secondary Day School in 1902/3 and in 1937 it became the So.Shields Girls Grammar School – same building, change of title. In the meantime, school lists show the changes. 1920: Westoe (secondary) boys, girls, infants. 1924: Westoe(secondary) boys, girls, infants. Westoe Central, boys, girls. (as from 1921) What isn't clear from the lists; was Westoe Central, boys, girls, housed in the newer Iolanthe Terr. building or in the older Westoe Schools on Chichester Road East? As yet all my enquiries haven't sorted that out.

*Letter from C.A.Willoughby* – he continues:
'In the 'Big boys' late 1920s, games in the school yard were the usual paddling a ball around in winter & cricket in summer. When the weather was decent we played games with cigarette cards – out of school we played marbles (alleys) in the back lane which bounded

the school on its high side. Small holes to hold marbles could be scraped out between the granite setts. Marbles came in four types: cheap pot – dirty white and easily broken, glazed white – more robust, and best of all a steel ball bearing. Glass ones with pretty colours weren't highly prized. The various games were handed down from one lot of boys to the next.
My last teacher in the junior school was Miss Barbour, a very diffident young lady with marvellous red hair. Then I left for the High School for boys – Miss Barbour was my 11 plus teacher.
I enjoyed my time at Laygate Lane: the most significant memory is of the grinding poverty that must have existed. But they were great lads and most of them no doubt would be caught up in the second world war.'

This next short excerpt should be in the thirties section but I place it here because it is a credit to both the school and the writer.

*Mortimer Road School*          *Built 1896, enlarged 1901*
*Fred Parkin*          *Started School 1929*

'My favourite toy was a tricycle... It was the cause of many grazed knees but I managed to stay alive until I began Mortimer Road Infants' when, after a few days, I wished I was back home risking the dangers of that three-wheeler.
Mortimer Road where I spent all my school-days...
I wasn't in love with school but there again, how many children were. Some subjects I excelled in, others were a disaster, algebra being one of them... Don't get me wrong, I wasn't a complete duffer. I was pretty good at maths, straight maths I mean and not bad at English. I didn't go to any High School but I was never out of the top section of an A stream class and left school near the top of X11A which was the highest class in the school and was also the last class of my school-days.
The teacher called me over to his desk.'Well Frederick,

I've been going through your school record & I find there are only a few scholars who have been at the school all their school-days & only hope you are not going to throw away those valuable years of education. Wherever your travels in the outside world take you I wish you the best of luck,' and with that he shook my hand and in so doing made me feel more grown-up than I had ever felt... The year was 1938 and the dark clouds of war were gathering.'

*from: This is My Life    Fred Parkin*

This example shows a well established and secure Education system in South Shields. The school kept records as a good school should, and Fred on his part took full advantage of the education available to him.

*Girls' High School 1945*
*From:School Days        Courtesy of Vera Kulkarni*
*(née Harrison)*

'I returned from evacuation in the Spring Term, 1945. I went to South Shields High School for Girls. It was a large three storey building; the classrooms opened out onto a large hall - a classic style for easy supervision.

Miss Dogherty, the Head, was feared by one & all. She was small, spoke in low tones but she carried such authority. We were waiting in line with hockey sticks, waiting for Miss Armstrong to escort us to the field. We started practising our song for the music class:

'My mother bids me bind my hair
With bands of rosy hue...'

Miss Dogherty came in by the gate, she pointed to Myra and me at the front.

'You girls, come to my room after games!'

I didn't enjoy my hockey that day. We waited outside her room. Myra was summoned first.

'What did she say?' I asked and Myra didn't tell me. She never did. Somehow, I was excused; maybe being small has its advantages!'    V.K.

## The Fourth Decade  1930–1939
### I receive a South Shields Education

In the 1930s there was a stability about South Shields schools. New schools were incorporated into an established system: Infant, Junior & Senior schools with scholarships for the Boys' High School, the Secondary School & Westoe Central. St.John's, an early higher grade school offered scholarships for subjects with a more commercial basis, also the Art School.

*C.A.Willoughby continues his account: Early 1930s South Shields Boys' High School, Mowbray Road.*

'I think the best way of doing this will be a 'Dramatis personae' of the staff involved and then talk about school life.
Headmaster: William T.Lucas 'Bill' – he lived 'above the shop' as it were – immediately opposite the school on Mowbray Road. Good at keeping order, commanding voice and well skilled in the use of the cane. After the last hymn at the morning assembly, he gave the blessing and if necessary read out the 'Black list' – names of boys who had committed such terrible offences that only the hand of 'Bill' himself could prevent them from following a life of sin.
Mr Hall, 'Tanker' He seemed to be deputy head – a well built and jovial man, always with a big smile. Taught some physics, music, and played the little organ for morning assembly.
Mr Wade. History, fearsome character, feared by the boys.
Mr J.D.Petty 'Jimmy' a very nice quiet character. An amateur astronomer: used to stay in the labs. at night to grind big lenses.
Mr Wesencraft 'Spuggy'; athletic frame, finely built, well known as a runner & assistant Scout Master.

Mr Griffiths – taught French and of course had to be 'Taffy'.
Mr Ellis 'Tarzan' I haven't the slightest idea why he was so called. A tall man, rather thin and a piercing high voice when roused.
Mr Cherry, 'Bob' I think from a boys' paper called The Magnet. He taught English and had a funny voice which I now hear every day – a Yorkshire man. A happy young chap – he used to have a three-wheeled car.
There was a Mr Joyce who taught physics and was referred to as 'Hopper Joyce'. He was a Scout Master & well-liked. He was in the Territorial Army so probably he vanished from the school when war broke out.
Mr 'Harry' Forrison, languages, rejoiced in the name of 'Joe Rock'. He was a bit of an Esperanto 'buff' and in hushed tones we used to say he was a 'Red'– not really knowing much about politics in those carefree days.
Two other teachers I recollect were Mr Revel and Mr Backhouse – the latter taught Latin. There was Arnold Josephs, geography, a famous football referee in his time. And, of course, the two ladies responsible for the 'little ones'; Miss Madden and Miss Malpas.'

C.A.Willoughby writes about 'caning':
'I cannot say that the cane was used with wild abandon – it was more a symbol of authority, wielded only in extreme cases. Most of the time it was waved about and banged on the desk to frighten... Those who used it were subject to much criticism from the 'lads'. Not for using it but the manner in which it was used... We also observed that some masters left the morning assembly before 'Bill' did his duty with the 'Black list'. Ah – yes – caning was an art form in those days. I can barely imagine a class of boys now without that symbol of authority in the corner.'

*The Search for Jigsaw Pieces Continues:*

Apart from the questions I started with, I found myself beset by simple questions with elusive answers. Again it was my curiosity about the history of my old High School on Iolanthe Terrace which led me to ask:

Prior to 1937 when this *building* became the High School for girls, was it also this *building* which housed the Westoe Central School? (I now know it wasn't)

I had the lists of schools in both Ward's and Kelly's directories. I could follow the changes in the *titles* of schools, (same school, same building, change of title) & I could work out dates when new schools entered the lists, but it did not specify which part of the Westoe School buildings *actually housed* Westoe Central.

Such a simple question and I thought a simple phone call would clear it. I turned to an early letter from C.A.Willoughby: 'My dear wife died – a lovely Shields girl and terribly missed. She went to Westoe Central and would have loved to write about the schools of Shields.' Charles Willoughby took the trouble to ring his wife's school friend 'Jenny' who confirmed they were both at Westoe Central in the early thirties but I couldn't ascertain from the answer the exact building. Neither could the friend recall Westoe Central for Boys although the school lists show both girls and boys.

A phone call to Ron Drew confirmed both boys and girls at Westoe Central but wasn't able to confirm which of the school buildings housed the girls: Westoe Schools (1891) on Chichester Road (East) or the end spur on Iolanthe Terr. or my old High school on Iolanthe Terr. which was built as a higher grade school in 1896. It would have been very easy to leave the bare facts (p21) & gloss over my larger question: If the Boys High School on Mowbray Road was established by public enterprise in 1885, then when and where was an equivalent school for girls established? I thought I'd found my answer in 1921 when Westoe Central was incorporated into the *existing school buildings* of Westoe Schools. I think I can imagine the two and fro of the discussion for this seems to me only half a solution; little more than a change in title. *Not even a new school for girls and I am beginning to suspect, not even being allowed to use the better equipped building on Iolanthe Terrace.* I'd taken it for granted that the Girls' Westoe Central school would have occupied 'my' school prior to 1937. That is why I'm still making phone calls about this small piece in the jigsaw.

The argument must have rumbled on within the Education Committee. It explains 'It is suggested that a new secondary school for girls be erected at Harton, and that the present High School for boys be extended to make room for 450, instead of 280 scholars.' This comment comes at the end of: *Early History of Educ. in South Shields up to 1930: G.Ernest Greenwell M.A.* and is Reference Only.

We know now that boys from the Mowbray Road High School, moved into the new school at Harton with the title, 'Grammar School' in 1937 and likewise, a new 'gym' & a flat for Domestic Science was added to the school on Iolanthe Terr. (still with outside toilets) and it became the Grammar School for Girls. As a Higher Grade school built to cover Science subjects it was well equipped on the top floor with the necessary labs.

If I say that decisions appear to favour 'boys' when in fact they are based on logistics rather than the influence of left-over attitudes from the early part of the century, then I stand to be corrected. Overall, South Shields has an excellent Education record.

I am now dealing with 'first hand accounts'; my own & Ron Drew's for he was actually at the High School in the change and notes the title 'Grammar School'. (p29) Yet another question looms. In 1941, my father, after years of unemployment, now had a regular wage as a ship's carpenter in the now busy shipyards. Even though I passed 'The Scholarship' fees were payable on a sliding scale and my mother with some pride declared earnings (average £5?) and in the first year paid possibly £10 a term. After that first year the fees were discontinued and my sister in 1943 paid none. Was the title 'Grammar School' linked with fee-paying?

Why do I query the title 'Grammar'? In 1945 Miss Dogherty, in assembly announced, that in line with the 1944 Ed.Act we were designated 'Secondary' rather than 'Grammar' school. Why do I remember Miss Dogherty's announcement? It was a small snobbery on my part and reflected on myself at eleven – so proud to pass for the 'Grammar School' – (and one of the lucky ones!) I think that at the same time, Senior schools were designated 'Secondary Modern' – a new title. That said, we continued to use the familiar Grammar/High School title.

Just a small point but such changes can be confusing when following the history of South Shields schools.

*1938*

High School (boys), W. T. Lucas, M.A. master. High School (girls), Miss A. Dogherty, mistress; W. Armstrong (boys) mstr; Miss E. Stenhouse (girls) mistress; Miss N. Fair (infants) mistress. Westoe Central, F. M. Hudson, B.A. (boys) master; Miss M. A. Barber, B.LITT. (girls) mistress. St. Stephen's, A. W. McGillivray, master. Stanhope rd. G. Cowan, master; C. H. Scott, mstrss; W. J. Davison (junior boys) master; Miss I. Bullock (junior girls) mstrs; Miss J. E. Atkinson (infants) mistress. Mortimer rd. R. Whitfield (boys) master; Miss A. R. Riddle (girls) mistress; Miss R. Metcalf (infants) mstrss. St. John's Senior, C. Barrass, master. Mowbray Junior, J. E. Murray, mstr. Voluntary Schools—West Har-

*Ward's 1940 p311*

High School (boys), W. T. Lucas, M.A. master. High School (girls), Miss A. Dogherty, mistress. Westoe, W. Armstrong (boys) master; Miss E. Stenhouse (girls) mistress; Miss N. Fair (infants) mstrs. Westoe Central (senior mixed) F. M. Hudson, B.A. master. St. Stephen's, J. G. Edgar, master. Stanhope rd. G. Cowan, master; C. H. Scott, mstrss; W. J. Davison (junior boys) master; Miss I. Bullock (junior girls) mstrs; Miss J. E. Atkinson (infants) mstrs. Mortimer rd. R. Whitfield (sen. mixed) mstr; Miss A. R. Riddle (jun. mixed) mstrs; Miss R. Metcalf (infts.) mstrss. St. John's Senior, C. Barrass, master. Mowbray Junior, J. E. Murray, mstr. Voluntary Schools—West Harton C.E.F. F. Ramsay, mstr; Miss D. E. H. Smith, mstrs. Holy Trinity C.E. Commercial rd. T. Thompson, master;

Simonside C.E. Simonside, Miss M. Welch, mistress. Cleadon Park Infants, Miss A. Henderson, mstrss. Cleadon Park Open Air; Miss E. C. Smith, mistress. Cleadon Park Partially Sighted, Mrs. E. Steele, mstrss. Cleadon Park, W. J. Rutherford (junior boys) master; M. A. Barber (senior girls) master; Mrs. M. S. Thompson (junior mixed) mistress. Harton, J. R. Stephenson (junior boys) master; Miss M. T. Christie (junior girls) mistress; Miss L. Davis (infants) mistress. V. C. Carter, sec. to the Education Committee, Town hall, Westoe rd

Harley G. Miss, 34 Central av. (T. 926)

Marine School, 13 Ocean rd. (T. 486); J. Hargreaves, principal

South Shields School of Art, St. Michael's av. north; E. Gill, art master

36

*A few more questions answered.*
Childhood leaves us a legacy of minor puzzles.
I started school in 1935. I lived on the corner by the pillar box; a short walk along Park Avenue would take me to Cleadon Park Junior School, but at five years old it was a long walk along King George Road, then Laburnum Avenue into the cut to the Infant School. I was an 'infant' and should go the easier way? Another puzzle was the way school friends disappeared – on the register one minute and gone the next. Oddly enough, one or two of these have been cleared up as I checked through the school lists.
In 1938 half of my class 'disappeared'. I don't think I ever put into words the loss I felt. I knew vaguely that they'd gone to a new school but on the phone to my brother last evening, he (amazed I didn't know, he too remembered losing half his class) told me they'd transferred to Harton. I rechecked the 1938 lists and a new school at Harton didn't show up – only memory recorded it. However I was very pleased to clear up a question which had hovered in the back of my mind since childhood. (1940 Harton: M.T.Christie,L.Davis)
My brother still lives in South Shields on Mowbray Rd. I had just pasted in the photo of the 'boarded up' High School. I rang and asked him if the school was still there? 'No. It was used as the Girls' High School annexe, then Teacher Training & finally there were plans for a hospice, but it was vandalised then demolished.' All in all, a very useful phone call.
With further questions in mind, I turned to *Ward's* for facts. Early in this century, schools were built to keep pace with industrial housing. My Grandfather Erickson lived in H.S. Edwards St. I was fascinated to see that 1897/8 H.S. ended at 76. 1903/4 F.Erickson craneman, lived at 63. 1905/6 H.S built to 148, 1907/8 H.S. to 294. Early lists show new streets and new schools. (p6/7, Gilbert St.p18, & maps p14/15)

*Cleadon Park Infant and Juniors     Built 1926/1928*

Of particular interest to me was the history of Cleadon Park school. It followed the same pattern: housing then schools. The foundation stone of Cleadon Park Estate was laid in 1920. The first mention of the Infants' School was in 1926. When the Junior School was built it showed up in the street lists: 1932, Park Avenue, Council school. ('my' school)

I can describe the long wooden building with its large 'baby' room at one end, a long corridor with a large doll's house which had tempted me to start school. Hopes of playing with it had faded by the time it was brought into a classroom and the teacher displayed each tiny piece of furniture to the class. One of life's little disappointments.

Starting school must have made a strong impression on me; the small incidents I remember are clear in the mind. I remember the squeak of pencils on slate, the fresh smell of real straws, choosing a thin straw as the fat ones disintegrated when drinking our milk and going as a class to the outside toilets – I seem to remember half doors and thinking it 'not right' if any girl insisted on leaving the door wide open.

One of the basics of learning, the vowels: a,e,i,o,u.

At the top of each blackboard in the first classes were five identical chalk pictures: a solid chalked apple, an egg in an egg cup, an overturned bottle with a pool of ink, a glowing orange, & a beautifully drawn umbrella. Months later I caught sight of the headmistress, Miss Henderson (?) redrawing the chalk pictures. I was filled with wonder – such fixed points in the class-room, felt more like the work of God!

I cannot say for certain, I understand the background training of teachers in the twenties & thirties – that is a study in itself. I did notice in the school lists that heads of larger schools had letters after their names, (see Westoe Schools) and *Pears Cyclopaedia, J16,* gave an overall view of Education but did not cover precise training provision. *Froebel & Montessori* methods were mentioned & in fact when I trained as a teacher (1968-1970) my tutor was *Froebel* trained, knew exactly what she was talking about and didn't neglect the three R's! I feel that my own early teachers were very experienced and shared a common pool of accepted practices. I would guess as teachers or heads moved from school to school, that the pattern of the school day, the teaching of the three R's, the 'gym', the hymns and songs, would be very much alike throughout South Shields and allowing for regional differences, similar throughout the country. (That's a very big 'Guess'.)

I remember the excitement of a new reading book – was there a Mrs Vinegar and pictures of green clad little men? also the boredom of class reading, thumbing ahead to read the story but keeping a finger on the line in case I lost my place when it came to my turn.

I was in top infants, Miss McQuillan's class and she was explaining tens and units. There was a '1' in the ten's column and a '9' in the unit's. 'Why would it be better to chose those many sweets?' she asked and pointed to the one. I put my hand up, sure of my answer; 'Because it would be greedy to chose the nine!' was ready on my lips. I wasn't picked and when the penny dropped, for it did, I can't explain the feeling of relief that my wrong answer hadn't been found out.

In the Juniors' 1938, Miss Anderson was my first teacher; dark hair, attractive, wore make-up! Then Miss H. who caned a long line of girls if their hands weren't clean for needlework. In the days of coal fires, there was a good bit of grime about. Now, 'tide-marks' are a thing of the past!

Miss Bailey was my teacher for the two scholarship years. She was very strict, a very good teacher, but I was quite afraid of her. I couldn't understand why she always scolded, a very quiet child at the bottom of the class. I still remember her name. Thanks to Miss B. nearly all the class passed the Scholarship. Looking back I always believed her 'scolding' was her way of controlling the rest of the class. However a recent letter from a school friend interested me greatly.

*Peggy Atkinson (née Shiel) writes:*
'Miss Anderson, who, like you, I remember being very well made-up, which was quite unusual in those days for a teacher. Mr Coxon who taught us to knit sea boot stockings for the sailors. (The wool was oily and hard, and hurt our fingers after a while.) Miss Clarke who got the whole class through the Scholarship to the High Schools. I have memories of her because she was kind although I once got the cane for fighting in the classroom! She also used to come to school in the morning on occasions wearing a suit with a modesty vest at the neck and go behind the blackboard and change into a blouse. We all knew what she was doing, it wasn't a perfect hiding place. This has always stuck in my memory!'

Such clear remembrances and moments, show how the teachers we had when young live on in our memories. They are tributes.

Peggy was a year ahead of me at school. Passing the Scholarship was an aim and a matter of pride. Miss Clarke's success was a triumph and we were the next class to sit. Miss B. was ambitious for the whole class, strict, and the unfortunate child, bottom of the class, may have been a constant irritation – perhaps.

*Harton Infant & JuniorSchool            Built 1938*
*Lies between Centenary Ave. & Prince Edward Road*
My Grandad often took me for a walk to see the new houses being built. The sight of door frames and no walls gave me a strange feeling and I would soon ask to see the upturned boat cut to make a potting shed on the allotments – they too would disappear. Harton

school would be built at that same time. (1938)
*Mary Roper, now Mary Whale*  Harton Infants'
'It was a long walk up the 'Red Road' as we called it.(Centenary Avenue) I was very tired walking to school on that first day. There were no buses as they hadn't finished building the estate. Most of the girls cried when their mothers left them but I didn't, I was more interested in the colourful building bricks & later on, you couldn't get me out of the toy shop. After having a bottle of milk, I fell asleep and remember the teacher shaking me...'

*Barnes Road, then to Dean Road*  1930s
*Sheila Devine, now Henderson*
In 1938 Sheila was at Barnes Road. Miss M.Shaw, headmistress, was very stern. There were prayers and singing first thing but she best remembers play in the school yard: Hitchy Red Rover: 2 teams, arms folded, hop on one leg and push each other. Leave-a-go: one starts chasing, first caught joins hands until long chain and all caught. In Barnes Road Junior School she was taught: Dancing round the Maypole.
'In 1939 she moved to Dean Road, Miss Cruickshank, Mistress. Domestic Science was in the 'flat'. They made aprons & hats; then washing and ironing one week and cleaning the next. Cooking: taking ingredients then hygiene, table settings, & later there was homework.'
'Teachers remembered: Miss Georgeson, very young, would blush over any rude words which came up.
Miss Hall, in music would stand with hands cupped under her big bosom, played records: Pier Gynt Suite. Singing lessons: Round-singing, London's Burning, White Sands, Grey Sands, & Who is Sylvia - Miss Young was a Tartar, used to rap you on the back of head with her ring.'
These are some of the things which are remembered & it all sounds very familiar as if the same patterns of the school day were being repeated in many other schools.

'In 1939 Dean Road was part-time. There was a bomb disposal unit nearby and a barrage balloon tethered by Deans Hospital.' Sheila went to school; mornings to Mortimer Road then a ½d transfer tram ticket to Cleadon Park School for afternoons. 'To reassure others in the air-raid shelters, Betty Sigsworth who had a lovely clear voice would sing one of the songs of the day: Amapola, my pretty little poppy.'
Yes, that too is a shared memory.
*South Shields High School for Boys     1936*
*Built at Harton   Cost £60,000*

*In 1937 the boys from the High School, Mowbray Road were joined by boys of Westoe Secondary: total 650.*

*Cleadon Park Senior School*  *Built 1938*
*Sunderland Road*

*Master of senior boys: W.J.Rutherford. Mistress of senior girls: M.A.Barber (from Westoe Central)*
It is to the credit of the So. Shields Educ.Committee that schools were built to meet the needs of the town & this was a fine new school for Senior boys and girls. Because Cleadon Park Juniors were mixed, I always thought that the Seniors were mixed too. Not so...

At this point I pored over *Ward's* School Lists to see how these new schools; the school at Harton 1936, & Cleadon Park built 1938, fitted into the Education system. I had photocopies of 1926, 1930, 1934, 1936, 1938, & 1940.
1926 showed Cleadon Park Infants only. Memory confirms that 'my' Cleadon Park Infant School was housed in sturdy wooden buildings. The Junior School was built later & shows up in the 1932 list. Mr Rutherford is master of Juniors (mixed) in 1934 & '36. In 1938 alterations indicate some change (It does not

specify the new senior school) but in 1940 Mrs Thompson is now mistress of Cleadon Park Juniors (mixed) just as I remember it and Mr Rutherford now master of the senior boys at the new school.

Memory again sheds light on the facts and figures. Miss Bailey was a dedicated teacher; I think that is clear. Mr R. her old head was replaced by motherly Mrs Thompson. Mr R. was an imposing figure, autocratic in a Victorian way. Occasionally he would call in to visit Miss B. A class of mixed 10 and 11 year olds would be pretty astute. They would see this stern, elderly teacher colour up and smile, and it just needed one to joke & whisper 'There's her boyfriend.' and everyone said it. Of course no truth in it, but in an old fashioned way I do feel he was her 'Champion'.

Up to this point, 1900 to 1940, I've tried to give a picture of Education in South Shields; not just listing schools & dates, but trying to show the people behind the facts and attempting to solve questions which arose. My effort to find which part of Westoe Schools housed Westoe Central for girls was solved by chance. I'd had flu, Doris Robson rang to ask how I was. I spoke of 'schools' & Westoe Central. 'Why their school was over the wall to ours, we could hear them!' So by word of mouth and not from the 'lists' I found out that Westoe Central for girls was in the end building on Iolanthe Terrace directly facing my old High School.
Days later, on the phone, Lilian Davison, a pupil at the school in 1938 confirmed it as a fact. At last!

The other point I think worth commenting on, was the feeling of 'awe' we had for teachers. We took our own fears to school, but this overall feeling of high regard for education was prevalent in the town as a whole and in my own experience, this respect and regard lasted all through my school days. (1935–1946)

*The Fifth Decade*                         *1940- 1949*
*Wartime, but Education Continues...*

In the early days of war there was the disruption of the national scheme to evacuate children to safer areas. For the children left behind, safe schooling was the next priority. In 1939, instead of going back in September at the end of the summer holidays, to my great joy, school was suspended while brick air raid shelters were built at the edge of the school yard parallel to King George Road. Many other schools were part time and when we did return to school, other schools with their own teachers used some of our classrooms vacated by the children who were evacuated. In no time our school days were back to normal except we had gas-masks at our sides and occasionally there would be gas-mask practice. In our desks was emergency food (often in red square OXO tins) should an air raid be prolonged so keeping us in the school shelters. Many children will remember, not so much the tins but the temptation of the biscuits and chocolate inside. Perhaps some children resisted but many more had empty tins in their desks. One more memory: because of a loss of schooling, the form of the scholarship was changed to a type of IQ Test rather than arithmetic and composition. I seem to remember feeling 'rushed' when Miss Bailey introduced us to an example of what was ahead. We, as a class had spent many hours breaking down 'problems'. Some things stick in the mind: in South Shields, ninety Girls' High School places were available. I came off badly with the new test. I was 92nd out of 93 places – just made it! I remember too the boy who passed in top place, whose father would not allow him to take the place offered. Young as I was, I felt for that boy.

This was 1941. Thoughts of war were pushed to the back of our minds & I travelled every day by tram to Victoria Arches, then up the bank past Westoe Schools, & not a thought in my head about their history!

*'Up the creek without a paddle'*     *Forties continued.*

The first four decades of this short history have leaned heavily on the school lists in both *Ward's & Kelly's Directories*. 1940 is the last available to me. From now on I must rely mainly on facts in my own memory, and first hand accounts from family and friends, cross checking whenever possible. Gordon Houlsby pointed out how perceptions differ. Two people could be at the same event yet describe it very differently.
I was always looking for links. Charles Willoughby writes: 'Art lessons were taken by a Mr Gill – a wiry rather nimble gentleman who could pitch you out of the room in a flash. He had quite a mass of hair and I suppose would have made a good Mephistopheles in an opera – he looked like the devil but was probably quite a nice gentleman.' Some fifteen years later Mr Gill from the Art School taught both my sister and myself at the High School. Silver haired, quiet, gentlemanly, slightly florid complexion. Puzzled I rang my sister & b-in-law who also remember Mr Gill & what C.W. describes could have been the last rebellion of the 'artist' before finally becoming conventional. It was then, Gordon pointed out, people's perceptions can be very different.

I started with a bright red folder and nothing in it. Now it bulges with lists, maps, & letters which form the basis of 'schools' from 1900. Other wallets contain photographs & memories which will make up 'schools' from the 1940s to the end of this century.
Apart from dates and names of schools many of the teachers are named in the memories. Quite often people remember an instance of bullying but it would unfair to give only those instances when there are other memories which have less punch but which are more representative of that great army of dedicated teachers. Nick-names crop up time and again. Occasionally they

are a bit inappropriate but usually they are enjoyable and should be accepted as such. That said, this history continues.

In 1945, I collected 'Confessions' in an old exercise book. I have about ten, very innocent and in very faint pencil. Just favourite flower, film-star, film, friend sort of thing - but of interest now, f. lesson, teacher. Miss Clarke is named, a nice tribute. Two girls born in 1928, both went to Cleadon Park Senior School and both name a Miss Reed, & a Miss Harrison is named. From the High School I named Miss Armstrong and friends named Miss Brewis, Miss Whately, & Miss Martin. I often heard boys at Harton Youth Club mention teachers at the Boys' High School. In the exercise book, C. Constable is mentioned twice, then a Mr Newby, an F.G.Grey, a Mr Chapman, and finally Gus. and Basher! Games lessons were either loved or loathed, much as expected and other subjects were spread pretty evenly. I was a bit disappointed not to find any links with the 'Dramatis personae' of Charles Willoughby. I felt Mr Wesencraft 'Spuggy' rang a bell but I may be able to make a phone call or two, and failing that I do have a little more about William T.Lucas ('Bill') for a later decade.

Perhaps I should do a 'Dramatis personae' of teachers I remember 1941 to 1946. My first impressions are the most vivid when it was 'School' with a capital 'S' but at 14 I joined the Youth Club which became all important and teachers began to blur into the background.

Miss Pinnington, (music) would discreetly return her handkerchief to her knicker leg, lady-like.

Miss Turner, (art) enthusiastic, but was made to toe the line and wasn't at the school long.

Miss Robinson, (French) tall, grey haired and stately, never needed to raise her voice.

Miss Murray, (Geography) quiet, reserved & well liked ensconced on the top floor in the geography room.

Miss Clish, (English) New, young, fairish naturally curled hair, tall and enthusiastic no nonsense, likeable.
MissV.Harrison (Latin &.RE) Wore smart dresses, carried herself well. A girl sitting beside me whispered that her mother said Miss H. always wore maternity style dresses; a most puzzling remark – and I pondered over it later. Teachers have a lot to put up with!
Miss Matthews (History) Young, attractive and liked teaching, nice atmosphere in class, & we worked hard.
Miss Martin (PE) well liked by the athletic girls but less agile girls had reservations. (myself & my sister)
On the top floor of our High School on Iolanthe Terr. were the labs. We studied General Science: Physics, Chemistry & Biology. Mrs Brewis, large, gentle, well-liked and Miss Stewart, smaller grey-haired, serious, worked hard to teach us what we needed to pass School Certificate.
In primary school I worked hard and always felt I did well. Although I just scraped into the High School, in Miss Bailey's class I was in top class & top of the girls. Because I had passed 92nd I went into C stream, came top, passed in to B stream and by the end of the year I was in the A class. There I came up against the very bright scholarship children, was no longer top and thereafter I still worked hard but kept a low profile.
I mention all this because 1, it gives some idea how the scholarship system worked in South Shields Education & 2, how behaviour in school developed over the years. I've said before how the presence of Miss Dogherty had such a controlling influence; she taught geometry with a sureness, walking back and forwards in front of the class, hand on hip and every pupil fully attending.
Miss Ditchburn (maths) Firm, well-liked, Guide Leader, fearsome? I always behaved, was quiet and 'good' in the 'Miss Bailey way'. On my report Miss D. wrote: 'Should take a more active/ co-operative part in class.' I was fifteen and she hurt my feelings.

*High School for Boys      Courtesy of Alan J.Atkinson*

*Sixth Formers 1946: Alan Atkinson, back row, third from the right. Norman Gedling, Albert Lombard (Losh) Michael Dinning (Mickey) John Erickson (my first cousin) et al.*

I turn now to a letter written about two years ago. It captures family concerns, the friendships of school, 'Spuggy' & the Gang show and adds a warm memory to the figure of W.T.Lucas, Headmaster.

*School Remembered.      Courtesy of William T.Lugton Extracts from a letter.*

'Born 1929. I was very young and can't remember anything about it. I remained very young for quite some time until my presence at Stanhope Road school was requested by the 'School Board' man. So there I went until over nine years of age...

My family moved to Cleadon, to Acacia Grove. Honesty

was instilled in our make-up thanks to a Ma whose Christian faith never flickered and we never ever resorted to dishonest actions to relieve the strain of poverty. I attended Cleadon Park Juniors' for one school year before moving on to the High School for Boys in 1940 at the age of eleven. I have a recollection of being hauled in from a playground fight by a Mr.Coxon; a tubby male teacher with a loud rather rasping voice, – that was at Cleadon Park Juniors...

My father died during my first year at the High School. He'd been ill for a long time. I managed school reasonably well but cannot say that I ever enjoyed it. I joined the Scouts run by 'Spuggy' Wesencraft and took part in the Gang Show: Gilbert & Sullivan's H.M.S. Pinafore. I used to walk to school with Tommy Fox & Frank Gray practising our French and German homework. Frank was always in command of his school work, quietly and modestly brilliant even then.

At the High School I became very good friends with Melv Murdoch and also was terribly shocked at the tragedy of his death...

Much of our school holidays and spare time were spent cycling. Rickie, Doug Atkinson, Colin Cook, Alan Cuthbert and all. Lake District, over the border, South to Yorkshire, and Stratford. Happy days spent on virtually traffic free roads.

An opportunity to begin an apprenticeship at the age of sixteen and to actually start earning some money was too important to miss, our financial situation being what it was, so I left school Easter 1945. Mr W.T.Lucas (I always liked him because he had the same initials as me – what an odd lad I was) Headmaster, was shocked as this meant missing school cert in the summer. He insisted that I shouldn't miss it and made the necessary arrangements – I had to return at exam time. (My attempts to miss the exam were thwarted by his superior and cunning anti-exam-missing strategy) I

sat the exams and managed to matric. I eventually conceded gratitude for his concern and insistence because the matric. was a mandatory requirement for subsequent entry to a Durham University Degree Course in Elec.Engineering which both Doug Hay and I attended at Sunderland Tech. College. Harry Shotton too but I believe he took the Mech.Eng.Course.'
*High School for Boys           Courtesy of Alan Atkinson*

*1946: Alan, just visible, centre at the front. Far back, Melv Murdoch laughing, & Graham Duncan. Robin Armstrong, Kenny Crawford, Michael Dinning, Alan Lombard, Bruce Jorden, Stan Archbold, et al.*

I searched out a second letter from Graham Duncan & asked both 'Lugs' & Graham if I could use extracts. Graham too was at the Boys' High School in 1945. As pupils, many of us could push the war into the back of our minds but when close family members were in the forces – thoughts of war came very close.

*From 'Aspects of War'   Courtesy of Graham Duncan*
'Being ten years old in 1939 meant that my formative years, to the age of sixteen, were to be spent during a major war... I was still alive to collect shrapnel, to watch dog fights, to investigate bomb damage; and to offer prayers to ensure that an air-raid would continue past the point which allowed absence from school until the following afternoon. Boys of 10 are indestructable. I remember no real problems until March 1943.
This was a bad month for us. It was then that a much loved uncle was lost at sea... War was no longer a moving picture; at fourteen, war was real and unfair. I recall a feeling of intense sadness and an immediate hatred of all things German... It was at this time that, for me, the aspect of war changed.
I now wanted the war to last long enough to allow me to be involved. This wasn't to be, as the war ended when I was sixteen. I was almost old enough to fight and I wanted to. I felt, in 1945, that I had missed my war, that my father and brother had had theirs and I had been denied my right.'
Although school isn't specifically mentioned, by inference, such strong thoughts developing in young minds must have made it very difficult for them to concentrate on work and exams. I think it is a point worth making.

*Cleadon Park Senior School        Flora Rutt née Roper*
'I was born in 1932. In 1939 we moved to Druridge Cres. I was at Cleadon Park County Secondary School & it catered for Horsley Hill, Sutton Trust and Cleadon Estate. I left school at Christmas 1946 – there were just a few of us, as all the others had left at Easter.'
The school leaving age was fifteen but many pupils, if they saw the opportunity to secure a job, would leave at Easter. Flora remembers an upsetting incident in a Cooking and Domestic Science lesson.
'I was making Eve Pudding and custard when Miss C.

came up behind me and said 'What do you think you are doing girl.' 'I'm mixing the custard Miss.' 'You're not doing it right, you're supposed to be mixing it in the bottom of the bowl.' 'I am' I replied. Because I had answered her back she said, 'Don't be cheeky with me, get yourself down to the Headmistress.'
I knocked on Miss A's door. I waited for her to say, 'Come in.' I then sobbed out my story to her. She smoothed things out saying, 'Dry your tears and go back to your class.' I went back to my class room but I happened to bang the door shut. I had rebelled. Miss C. shouted again, 'Go out into the corridor and come back in but close the door quietly.' 'No I won't.' I couldn't believe it was myself answering her back! 'What did you say girl. How dare you.' I still stubbornly replied, 'I do dare and I am not doing it.' Her cold eyes & her words upset me. 'If you ever get married, you will live out of a frying pan.'
I debated about this; these confrontations do happen but I think it illustrates the tensions of puberty, the difficulty of control for both teacher and pupil, and at times there is flare up.

*Cleadon Park County Secondary School*
*Mary Whale née Roper*                   *1945 to 1946*
'Cleadon Park Senior School was the most modern, up-to-date school. It opened in 1938. I recall a lot of strictness there. I was 12-13 years old, just after World War Two. The Headteacher was Miss Aitchison. There were separate classes for boys and girls.'

*School Dinners*
'On one occasion, Miss- was in charge. She was strict and feared by the girls. There were eight of us sitting at a long wooden table. The mince wasn't very nice and we left some on our plates. Miss- shouted, demanded we eat it all up. We were terrified... I remember her harsh voice saying: "When it comes to eating your sweet and 'seconds' you have no bother at all."

I think it was due to the fact, that food was still short and rationed, and nothing should be wasted, but...'
*Photograph: Courtesy of Mary Whale née Roper   1948*

*Head:Miss Aitchison on the left. Mary Roper, 13 years old, tall, in back row, marked with an 'X'*
*Names of other girls: Nelly Jeffery, June Emmerson, Vera Ovington, Joyce Leather, Irene Hudson, Lillian Chavener, Jean Armstrong, Doreen Holmes, Margaret Wade, Olive MacAlister, May Groggins, Marcella Clark, Lillian Ford, Jenny Richardson, Beryl Houghton, Louie, Margaret Elliot, Joan Mackins, Joyce Bone, Doreen Jeffles, Lilian Charlton et al.   (39 girls)*

Mary Whale continues her story:
'There is another memory relating to school dinners & about receiving the dreaded cane. Often after dinners we were allowed to play out, or go to the sweet shops on Park Avenue. One day, one of us came up with the idea of visiting Cleadon Hills for a change. It was summer and lovely and warm. Myself and two friends, Vera and Joan, enjoyed romping over the hills, played hide-and-seek amongst the rocks and gorse bushes,

until we realised we were going to be late. We ran all the way back to school, out of breath. We were caned, one by one in front of the class and I remember pulling my hand away each time the teacher tried to cane me. Miss– took hold of my wrist, only then did I receive a sharp rap on my hand three times, plus one hundred lines saying I must not be late in class. I didn't cry but tears welled up inside of me and after that I was never late again.

'Daddy' Milne was a well known figure in the boys' school. He was a tall, thin man with wire spectacles. He always carried a long, hooked, thin stick.

In very cold weather we (the girls) were made to strip down to our regulation navy blue knickers and white vest. My knickers always seemed to have a hole in them, having been passed down to me by my sisters. I enjoyed playing netball in the yard and could easily score a goal having the advantage of being tall.

Four single brick pillars divided the yard. Occasionally the ball would stray into the boys' half & one time I ran into their yard to fetch it back. The boys heads all turned to see me in my knickers & I was very embarrassed. Next I recall the noise of 'Daddy' Milne's thin stick and his voice as he shouted, 'Look this way.' Those sounds remain with me yet.'

I've mentioned briefly how we take our fears to school with us. I made another phone call to my brother, John Erickson who was also at Cleadon Park Seniors: 'Was it a very strict school?'

He remembered 'Daddy' Milne and his stick was nick- named 'Ginger the Rod!' Yes, teachers were strict but most boys took it all in their stride; even 'six of the best' was a case of, grin and bear it!

*I Take a Walk*               *Monday 19.10.1998*

Quite a day today! Metro to South Shields. Called in at the library with a list of questions. In the Local History section, the librarian showed me some further source material & I photocopied their maps: 1936, 1948, 1974 – the outlines of schools appearing and disappearing over the years.
It was a lovely morning. I felt I'd seen too many 'lists', made too many phone calls, studied too many maps. I decided to take a walk.
First stop, St John's, on Beach Road. An elderly gentleman, passing, pointed out luxury flats where the school had been. 'My wife went to St John's, she was very fond of the school.' He then directed me towards Osborne Avenue. I skirted Westoe Cemetery and stopped in my tracks – *Candlish Street!* The street I'd checked for dates in the *'Lists'* from a remark made many years ago: 'You were born in Candlish Street.' I turned from my path and walked along the street – was it 68 or 70? I had my folder, checked the list: 1930, J.Corby, Fitter, at number 70. I knocked. No reply. What could I have said? – 'My Grandad lived here. I was born in this house.' but there was no reply and I walked on.
Just before Iolanthe Terrace I saw a piece of waste ground and a clear view of the sea. It was dark blue. The steps over the railway line had gone. Then I saw modern houses where once I'd spent five years of school-days. I spoke to a lady. 'Yes, Westoe Schools are down now except the infants' building.' She thought the old Boys' High School came down about four or five years ago. (1994)
I walked to my brother's house, Mowbray Road, in search of a cup of coffee. No one at home!
I retraced my steps and saw that the school field had shrubs, seats and a children's play area. *No Boys' High*

*School! No Art School!* The Lodge was still there and further along St Michael's Avenue I came to the last remaining building of the massive Westoe Schools built 1890/96: Westoe Infants' School. (Visitors straight to office please.) The atmosphere felt good; bright pictures and a class singing in the hall. I went straight to the office but was conscious that instead of a very large Victorian hall, it was smaller, more cosy. I asked a couple of questions but didn't stay long. Afterwards I remembered the children, cross legged in blue jumpers and would have liked a photograph.

I followed the familiar grey wall (from 50 years ago) down Chichester Road bank and saw that the corner shop was now converted to a house. During the war there were few sweets about and the shopkeeper sold half tubes of Horlicks tablets for sweet starved school children like me. Now just a memory... Alas.

*St John's Higher Grade School*

St. John's Higher Grade School, Beach Road.

*St.John's Higher Grade School  (see p6)*
St.John's was an early Higher Grade school before 1900 until it was displaced when Ocean Road and Westoe Schools were granted Higher Grade/Secondary status but it still retained its higher grade reputation. The school developed with a more commercial basis and an ex-pupil described it as having a 'vocational' tradition. In the 1940s it offered book-keeping, office practices, as well as art, dance and literary subjects. No school certificate but the very useful R.S.A. qualification. There was a selection process for entry. Classes on the whole had a preponderance of girls, possibly three quarters girls and a quarter boys. At the same time, the Art School, St Michael's Avenue, with Mr Gill as Art Master, had a selection process; boys & girls from St. John's & other schools could attend for art tuition. In this way, St. John's had its own place alongside the High Schools.
As has been said, St.John's School has gone, but it is still remembered with regard by ex-pupils. I heard a remark, 'Oh, students from there got jobs in the Town Hall!' but how true that is, I don't really know.

*School Memories       Courtesy of Muriel & Doug Hay*
*Cleadon Park Juniors' School*
'Mr Coxon remembered for his immaculately turned out 'portly figure' with a habit of pulling down his starched shirt cuffs.
After the exam results for the High School were published Miss Clarke brought him in to acquaint us with French which we would be taught at the High School. He spoke a little French to us and then talked of holidays he had spent in Europe – quite awesome to a little boy whose holidays up to then had been spent at Barnard Castle and Osmotherley!'
Boys' High School Characters:
'C.'Charlie' Constable who taught history. He delighted

in giving lines to anyone he caught resting their head on their extended arm – 'the weary weight of the brain needs no support from the arm' he quoted.

'Spuggy' Wesencraft, English & Gym Teacher & quite handy with a slipper which he used in lieu of a cane if necessary in the gym where flimsy shorts gave little protection.'

*William T. Lucas M.A. Headmaster High School for Boys Retired 1955*

MR W. T. LUCAS

'Bill' Lucas lived on Sunderland Rd. and had an agreement with his neighbour backing on to St.Mary's Avenue enabling him to cut through his garden to the school gates instead of walking right round. In the early years we had to wear school caps & he instilled in us the courtesy of 'doffing' our caps to him as he crossed the road & he, in return, raised his trilby – manners maketh the man! N.B. Basher & Fred Gray are the same person.' D.H.

*Cleadon Park Juniors' School      Muriel Hay née Gray*

'I remember Miss Clarke quite clearly. My other clear memory is being caned for talking during prayers in the hall and I was ashamed to tell my Mam as she had instilled in us a strong sense of good behaviour.'

*Girls' High School 1942...*

I was rather apprehensive when I started at the Girls' High School in 1942 as my two older sisters were there and I had heard them talking about Miss Dogherty the Headmistress, who seemed to strike terror into all her pupils, yet I discovered she had a kind streak.

One day the School Secretary came to our classroom to say Miss Dogherty wanted to see me in her room. I was terrified! However, she sent me to the Upper Hall where my Mam and Dad were waiting. He had come on leave and wanted to take his girls home and she allowed it. How proud we were of Dad in his Merchant Navy uniform.

Sadly, my beloved Dad was lost at sea in February. I couldn't do my homework that night and next morning my Form Mistress, Miss Watling who taught Maths, wouldn't let me tell her the reason privately, but made me stand up and tell the whole class. She then called me to her desk and spoke so kindly, apologising for making me cry. At the end of term she said I had done well under the circumstances.

I settled down well and enjoyed my years at High School.

*Cleadon Park Senior School 1946/47   John F.Erickson*
'I did not like school, on the other hand I did not hate it. When I was at school the leaving age was fourteen but in my last year it was raised to fifteen. I was able to leave at fourteen but given the option of going back if I had not found a job. We were told if we went back we would have no teacher and would have to teach ourselves.

About six of us who had not found jobs went back. We were given a small box-room with a couple of tables and chairs and then left to our own devices. As a bonus we were made prefects.

This spell at school for me was the only time I ever enjoyed it. After about six weeks I found a job as Office Boy in Readhead's and went on to serve my apprenticeship as a fitter.

I can honestly say that I never ever wished I was back at school.'

My brother John was 'persuaded' to write a memory for the book. After many starts he succeeded. He shows how schools needed time to adjust to the new school-leaving age & he puts into words an attitude to school which many people understand.

*The Sixth Decade*  *1950–1959*
*I depend on first hand accounts from others.*

In the early fifties I was working and had no close connections with schools. In 1952 I married and left South Shields to live in Newcastle upon Tyne. My brother John Erickson did not leave the town and now he and his family are able to answer many of my questions about 'schools'. Sometimes, on the phone after some comment of mine he will say, 'But surely you knew that school was demolished years ago!' and I just can't believe it.
To speak of schools being demolished is jumping the gun because in the 50s, it was still a time of austerity. There was no house building or new schools during the war years and after the war, the housing shortage was acute. New housing, new schools would be appropriate and not demolition. No doubt the education authority had reason to be thankful for the legacy of fine school buildings from the turn of the century. In the time of austerity, there would be peeling paintwork and plaster but the old fashioned classrooms with high windows and the halls with parquet flooring could still be used safely, until newer schools could be built.
 Barnes Road was just such a school, a very old school built as early as 1846/1850, with a proud reputation.
*Joan Steinson née Law  1953*
'I enjoyed my school-days. I enjoyed learning and actually having children to play with was heaven. I started at Barnes Road Infants' in January 1953. The headmistress was Miss Philips, a very remote figure. My first teacher was Miss Tingle, she was very young – ours must have been her first class and even today I remember her enthusiasm. On the day of the school photograph Miss Tingle must have been absent & Miss Philips is standing at the back. My friend Carol is in both photographs and we are still good friends.'

*Barnes Road Infants'  Courtesy of Joan Steinson*
*First Class 1953*

*Class photograph, 42 mixed infants. Joan is on the left end, second row from the front and Carol is fourth from the other end on the same row.*

'From the Infants' we moved to the adjoining building into the Junior School which was girls only. At eleven we merged with the boys once more and those of us who failed the eleven plus went to Dean Road Seniors. Going on to Dean Road Seniors we were reunited with the boys.

Most of the children in the photographs went right through the system with me and I still see several of them today.'

Barnes Road Infants'  Courtesy of Joan Steinson
Class of seven year olds 1955

Miss Philips, headmistress is on the left and Miss Wilkinson on the right. Joan is fourth from the left in the front row & her friend Carol is second from the left in the row behind. There are 33 'mixed' infants.

'The second photograph was taken before we went to the Junior School, where the boys were segregated from the girls. Miss Wilkinson on the right was to be our first year teacher.'

Joan writes that the photographs were taken two years apart. A look at the brick wall behind & it is the same in both photographs. Barnes Road celebrated over 140 years as a school; those same walls withstood countless children at play and now...Gone!

## South Shields Girls' High School 1947

*Teacher:Miss Goudie. Joyce Lambie, end R. back row.*
*School Memories          Joyce Erickson née Lambie*

'I remember Miss Goudie. Very gentle – I thought she was old – everyone's old when you're eleven. (She is still alive today & must now be very old) We bought her a cheap china brooch as a present. We thought this a bit of a lark – but were brought down to size when she said a public 'thank you' next day in assembly.
I started the Grammar School in 1946.(1946 to 1951) I was very proud to have passed, even though they weren't the happiest years of my life.
I was in a group of five friends known as the 'famous five' and we were always in hot water. We were threatened with letters to our parents. For weeks I would cycle home at lunch-time with heavy heart. I would look for a frown on mother's face or a brown envelope! This never happened but it really upset me.
Miss Dogherty was Headmistress when I started – she

filled me with fear – stood no nonsense. Dr Ramsden took over in 1949; she had the same control but did it with a smile.

In my third year they introduced the '13+'. I worked so hard – for the first time – because the bottom 10 were sent to secondary schools. I thought '13+' a bad idea.

Once we reached 14 we had a mixed Christmas dance at the Boys' Grammar School. The excitement reached fever pitch in the weeks leading up to it!

I wore an aunt's dress 'cut down' and felt like Marilyn Monroe. We went in a taxi. We had to wait for a friend because she had to shave underarm. I remember being quite shocked – I had no underarm hair! This was an age of innocence: dancing with boys, crushes, sending notes.

I remember Mr S. Art teacher. He was I think, the only male teacher. We would try to embarrass him with awkward questions and giggling. Poor man!

There was great rivalry between 'Houses'. I was in Yellow House and loved sport. We would cross the road to the playing field in our navy knickers. (Games skirts came later).

I left school totally unprepared for the workplace.' J.E.

In 1941 we had soft green gym outfits. By 1945 they weren't replaced. Wartime austerity lasted many years hence 'navy knickers' and 'make-do & mend' dresses.

*School Memories*          *Valerie Ross née Smith*
*Mortimer Infants' 1946 – 1952*
'During music lessons, we were all given instruments. I was given the humble triangle. How I longed to play something else. At last my great day came, and I was given a try on the cymbals. I hadn't realised how difficult it would be to get the crash in just the right place; my first attempt was rather muffled, at the second attempt I brought the cymbal down on the

wrong side and cut my thumb. It was back to the humble triangle again!'

*Mortimer Juniors 1948-1952*

'I was chosen to be part of the junior choir, this was taught by Miss Nancy Warren and we spent a lot of time learning Hansel and Gretel by Humperdink. I remember the choir was greatly praised by a visitor to the school. Miss Warren lives in Mortimer Road now and is organist at Westoe Methodist Church.

For the last two years in the juniors we had the same teacher who coached us for the eleven plus. This was Mr Ellis, my first male teacher. He used the cane every day and I was terrified of him. I see from my school reports that there were fifty-three in my class at the time. I passed for the grammar school...'

*The Girls' High School 1952-1957*

'I was studying very hard for my 'O' levels and one Sunday, I decided to sit out in the garden. It was very hot but I was determined not to miss the fine weather, so I sat out all day revising.

As I was putting my clothes on the next morning, I heard a loud ringing in my ears and the next thing I knew I came round on the floor. I had fainted and fallen on my nose and it was bleeding. My arms were badly burnt as I have a very fair skin. I still had to go to school however, but I had a very bad headache. I was sent to see the school secretary, Mrs Ogle, who gave me a couple of aspirins, (they were the school cure-all) and at lunch time I was sent home.

A week or so later everyone who was taking external exams was called into the upper hall and Doctor Ramsden gave us all a lecture about not sitting in the sun, using me as a bad example.

I did learn a hard lesson that day and have always kept my head and arms covered whenever the sun is hot.'

*Girls' High School     Courtesy of Val Ross née Smith*
*Valerie Smith: extreme left, 2nd row from back. 1956*

*South Shields Girls' High School 1956*

*An Overall View of the Fifties*
It was a simplification to view 'schools' as a 'jigsaw'. It is more a many layered canvas; each school a thread woven into the whole. Only a few threads have been followed: the organisation and building of 'schools' at the turn of the century; Westoe Schools; Laygate Lane *et al;* the High Schools, Westoe Central, St John's, and Cleadon Park – but so many more not covered.

And what of the new schools – after the famine of the war years, in the fifties, eleven new schools, not counting the extensions to existing schools because of overcrowding. The Education Authority was faced with

'a bulge' – births 1946 to 1949; a problem faced throughout the country. Also, new housing and movements in population caused further headaches.
Thornholme & Horsley Hill (1950) Redwell & Downhill (1951) Simonside & Garnett Infants'(1952) Biddick Hall (1957) Whiteleas & Cleadon Park open-air (1958) and Brinkburn Secondary School for 650 pupils (1957/9) Extensions to *Grammar-Technical* Schools, Horsley Hill, Redwell, Mortimer Road, & Cleadon Park Seniors'.

My interest in titles continues. Changes can be very confusing – following some thread it breaks and is picked up again under a different title.
Now we have *Grammar-Technical School,* yet another title to understand.
With the demand for extra places at the High Schools because of 'the bulge'; in 1953/4 a new technical wing was added to the Boys' High School at Harton. (£184,000) Also in 1953, girls from St John's School joined the Girls' High School, Iolanthe Terr. The two enlarged schools became *Grammar-Technical* Schools. Both schools could now offer 150 places, & by 1957 they could each offer 180, 11-plus & 13-plus places. While giving credit for the many new schools & the Education Authority's many problems, I feel frustrated as I record the following. To house the extra places, Dr Ramsden became Head of a four-part school: High School on Iolanthe Terrace, plus extra classrooms, the old Boys' High School, & the Art School, St Michael's Ave. The technical subjects were shorthand and typing in addition to normal grammar school subjects.
Dr Ramsden took over the headship of the Girls' Grammar School from the late Miss A.Dogherty in May 1949. She began as head of a traditional High School which was later enlarged on a split-site, & she still maintained the same high standards. Looking back I think Dr Ramsden deserved a medal!

*The Seventh Decade                  1960 to 1969*
*Ahead: Comprehensive Education & Computers*

I've already said, I moved to Newcastle in 1952. My two children were born in 1960 & 1963. Because of them, in the late sixties I followed all the 'discussions' about the change to 'comprehensive' schooling. It is now, very interesting for me to follow the moves in South Shields towards that change and recognise the same 'For & Against' points of view.

In 1964, the word 'comprehensive' began to circulate & doubts were cast on the 'fairness' of the 11-plus. By 1966 those in education circles were talking seriously about 'all-in' schools. The Council put forward a plan/s to teachers. Most parents were unaware of what was being discussed.

*Shields Gazette, Friday, August 5th 1966*
*Proposed: Six, 1,500-pupils; mixed secondary schools, catering for all children aged 11 to 18. These will replace the South Shields Grammar Technical Schools for boys and girls and the nine secondary modern schools. The 11-plus examination, introduced by the 1944 Education Act, will be abolished.*

Meanwhile, (1964) plans were afoot to build a *new school* at Cleadon Park to house the Grammar school girls – the split site at Westoe being far from satisfactory. In 1921, Westoe Central – *no new school;* 1937, Iolanthe Terrace – *no new school;* 1953 Split site – *no new school.* At last, 1964, the promise of a new High School for Girls.

It is ironic that at this same time, 'comprehensive' and the 'abolition of segregation at eleven' were just coming under discussion – as a consequence, the new High School at Cleadon Park (King George Road) was put on 'hold'. The following cutting tells it all.

*Shields Gazette, 21.7.1970 All-in Schools put on ice.*
(Secondary modern schools needed improvement before plans to go 'comprehensive' could go ahead – advice of Dept.of Education & Science. Probable change: 1973)
*Footnote: The Director of Education, Mr Geoffrey Denton, told the committee it had to pay a bill for £4,062 from Page, Hill & Reid, Architects, for work done in 1964 on the original plan for a new girls' grammar school.*
As the sixties rolled on, plans were drawn up, redrawn, teachers were consulted & the parents were informed.
In 1967 an interim plan was turned down by the Secretary of State & did not get the full backing of teachers. *'back to the drawing-board'.* In 1970 the redrawn but still controversial plan was again not accepted. Secondary modern schools would need to be improved to meet the standards of the 'All in' plans.

The good thing about this controversy was that the whole country explored educational change and reported successes & failures. In So. Shields there were plans to raise the school leaving age to sixteen. Secondary modern schools were revising exam opportunities: Cleadon Park Seniors' offered Northern Counties School Cert. & 'Humanities' In 1969 they installed 'computer apparatus' & linked with the Pegasus computer at the boys' grammar school. The 'Victorian' schools held prize giving and Jubilees. Despite opinions about 'old schools' Mr Irvine, Head of Dean Road upheld that the spirit of staff & children was more important than the structure. By 1969, senior schools offered careers advice and 'Work Experience'. The massive Westoe Schools still played its part. Westoe Secondary Girls' was popular with parents: its Head Mrs I. Keir introduced a tutorial system, despite poor conditions the school was 'small' 380 pupils, & 75% 'chose' to stay on. Westoe Secondary Boys' 350 pupils, 'not so go-

ahead academically but Mr Carr the Head knows all the pupils and has few disciplinary problems.'
Something tells me that 'small' is lost in 'All-in' plans. Indeed, studies talked of 'smaller' comprehensives with sixth form colleges to carry extra subjects.
It is good to record that South Shields continued to improve standards and introduce new ideas into schools even as they discussed plans for comprehensive education.

*Computers in Schools, Pegasus Arrives*       *1966*
*Shields Gazette 22.8.1966*
Mr Egner, Head of South Shields Grammar-Technical for Boys watched as Pegasus arrived from London in three haulage lorries!
The six year old computer worth £100,000 was given free to the Education Committee.
The following accounts express so well, what a milestone this was at the time.

*The Summer of '66*       *Courtesy of Alan Drew*
'I seem always to have been keen on football, although it was really brought on in the late '50s and early '60s when my father and his friend George Smith would often take me to Simonside Hall to watch South Shields. In 1963 I made my first of many visits to Roker Park, and a Sunderland supporter I have remained since.

Three events in 1966 were to have a major impact on my future. In June, I sat my GCE"O"Levels – quite a traumatic experience, especially as I was still just 15 years old. I did well enough to go on to the Sixth Form. The second event was, of course, England's World Cup victory in the July. It increased the popularity of football and I became confirmed as a football fan(atic?)
However, there was one more event taking place that

summer, which was both exciting, and expensive. The South Shields Education Authority had agreed to spend £2,000+ (installation costs) for a computer, for the Boys' Grammar School. When September came, and I entered the Sixth Form, there it was. The Ferranti Pegasus Mark 1V filled a classroom, and needed a full-time technician (Mr.Elliott) to keep it going. It ran on valves, drum storage, and paper tape, and was science fiction come true. Of greater significance to me, though, was the fact that it was the responsibility of the Mathematics Department – my main subject.

I took to Computing like a fish to water. Sixth Form life at the Grammar School contained an amount of free time, which meant that I had a near constant presence by the machine. I would be creating punched paper tape, correcting and splicing it, feeding it in, and then trying to make sense of the output.

Mr Dixon was the Head of Mathematics at the time, & was assisted in teaching Computing by a part time teacher Miss(Avril?) My interest, enthusiasm, & fast growing ability with the computer meant I was often allowed to 'do my own thing'. We often made music – literally! A speaker was attached, which produced a tone at a varied pitch according to the rate at which it looped through the computer program. My first serious project, not surprisingly, was to produce an updated football league table, which I published on a Monday morning.

I had three years in the Sixth Form, which enabled me to gain valuable experience with the system. More importantly, it gave me a sense of purpose when I went to University. I was going to become a computer programmer when I graduated.

And so it came to pass. I have been in Computing all of my working life, and have made a successful career out of it. The vision of the Education Authority members in 1966 is quite startling when you look back, and I will be eternally grateful to them. Although I no longer live in the North East, my career has given me the wherewithal to travel north every fortnight, and to have a season ticket at the Stadium of Light. The summer of '66 was indeed a key moment in my life.'

## Addendum to Summer of '66    Courtesy of Ken Drew

'Mr Egner, headmaster, was very advanced/futuristic for his time. I remember he made contact (& several visits) to colleagues in Norway to generate the school timetable *on a computer;* pretty advanced for 1965ish. He also arranged talks by visiting 'speakers'. A talk by Chris Bonnington: 'A Mountaineer' did not take my attention, even at his second visit!!

The Ferranti Pegasus did take up a lot of space. A classroom was cleared to make room for Power Bay, Mill & drum storage, and Central Suite with Operator's position. The key switches were just below the CRT readouts. When operated, you could see the working 'bits' (literally) of the commands and results. Outside the classroom a storage room was converted to the Electricity Distribution Room to accomodate the new electricity supply. As it was, the heat generated from all the valves must have been some 5 or 10 kW.

One particular program allowed us to key in numbers to represent notes; this opened up the 'musical' side of the computer. At the time, I was learning the guitar, so many tunes sounded quite good through its single 'voice'...      The technician, on average was able to provide a working computer 3 days out of 5.

I was impressed by a brother who could read the 5 hole paper tape by holding it up to the light, & spotting spelling mistakes! & generating a program which produced an updated Football League Table on a Monday morning...'

Ron Drew mentioned that his sons were at the High School in the 60s. Alan was 2 years ahead of Ken in the sixth form & they exchanged remembered facts about *Pegasus* via e-mail! Both sons are 'computer literate'. All three exchange e-mail. The sons 'teach' the father! The music link interests me. Ron composes music (notation!) using his computer & acknowledges the way his sons pass(ed) on their 'know-how'. It is worth remembering that all three men & countless others received an excellent South Shields education.

*A Personal View - Not Sour Grapes.*          *1967*
This study of *'schools'* has grown bigger by the day. I could have written a much larger book had I used more facts & less 'chat' but my original plan of 96 pages still stands. It has been a learning experience for me, more than that, it has been a voyage of discovery.
For instance, C.A.Willoughby's 'caning' p33 & MaryW' 'the dreaded cane' made me really think back. I did 'get the cane' for I would stiffen my hand & I remember a sting, but I associate this with the junior school, and we just accepted that teachers had canes.
It struck me, that at the High School, *I could not remember the cane.* I rang my sister Joan (née Erickson) and she, with some surprise remembered being called to Miss Dogherty's room, in trouble, but could not remember being caned! Joan rang Audrey P. She too remembered sitting outside Miss D's room 'shivering' but no cane, whereas in the juniors most teachers had a cane in the corner. Something tells me, it was a matter of pride: we were expected to behave and that was it. Miss D's policy was followed by the teachers – no canes – but never spelt out.
I think it can be said that a 'good' Headteacher is invaluable to a school. One of the threads I followed earlier: pen sketches of W.T.Lucas, confirm my view of him as an excellent Head. He retired in 1955, having

stayed on past his 65th birthday to oversee the £184,000 extension of this Grammar-Technical School.

I realise now that my choice of pen sketches of Miss Dogherty all stress her strictness. I detect some resentment on my part having been on the receiving end. It is the resentment of a teenager and I would like to set the record straight. Yes, the boys were moved to that fine new school at Harton and ours was a three story Victorian building, built in 1896. Thanks to Miss D. and her discipline we were given a first class education – good teachers who shared her standards were able to teach in quiet classes. My sister, not good at maths, grasped Geometry under Miss Dogherty's tuition – even now, I too like the clarity of Geometry.

In May 1949, Dr E Ramsden took over the headship from the late Miss N.Dogherty. (Ann/Nancy) The high standards were maintained by the new Head. The same control, ideals, traditions, & uniforms were retained.
*Girls' Grammar School head for 18 years retiring.*
*Shields Gazette 18.1.1967*
In 1953 (see p69) Dr Ramsden was given headship of the enlarged Grammar-Technical School for Girls, on a split site. I can only imagine, her efforts to maintain cohesion and discipline, as valiant. From hearsay she did just that for 18 years. However, there was a promise of a *new* Grammar School at Cleadon Park & in 1964 plans were drawn up.(see p74) The planned school was put on 'hold' and in the late 60s it was overtaken by plans that it should be a new comprehensive school. In 1967 Dr Ramsden resigned after 18 years holding the fort. She was in line to head the new Cleadon Park School! The change from single-sex to mixed and from grammar to comprehensive was no mean task. She foresaw it would require a headmistress to steer it throughout the change. She and her staff were praised

for attaining high examination results in face of 'difficulties'. A remark 'just a pity she won't be here to work in a glorious new building.' was probably well meant. In 1967 her successor, Miss G.Harris was announced so: Woman will steer girls school to 'All-in' system. 'A key post – has gone to a woman.' Thirty years ago, such remarks went by unnoticed. As to my question: 'When did girls have a school equivalent to that of the boys' High School?'
Three answers: *Never, or, 1937 to 1953, or, 'It's all water under the bridge!'*

*Eighth Decade                              1970 to 1979*
*Comprehensive Schools Established. Planned: Schools with Nursery units & purpose built Nursery Schools.*

By 1970 interim plans for the changeover were in place with 1973? as the date when South Shields would go 'comprehensive.' The plans were still controversial and open to change. Nine comprehensive schools. (Ocean Road & Baring Street Seniors' not used) King George Road (being built) & Harton Boys' – these two grammar schools would have sixth forms. Redwell, Cleadon Park, & Brinkburn would take 900 pupils but no sixth forms. Stanhope & Dean combined; would have 900 pupils. Chuter Ede School would take 600 pupils & Mortimer would have a new wing, again 900 pupils and no sixth form. *This plan was still open to alterations.*
Newcastle upon Tyne too, in order to make the change had a mix of purpose built, and older schools on split level sites. – Not an ideal solution but the same problem was faced in other towns and cities.

Faced with a surfeit of facts I needed some 'younger' voices. I turned to my nephew & nieces who were educated in South Shields. Janet speaks first.

*Grammar-Technical Girls' School 1970s*  Janet Erickson
*Dear Auntie Mary...*
I've been racking my brains all week for events in the 70s and rang my friend Ashley to confirm dates...
To begin with I went to Gilbert Street (1964) for a short while before moving to Oak Avenue & then began attending Harton Infants' followed by Harton Juniors'.
I do remember the period coming up to the 11+. For most people this was a big event & I had really set my heart on passing it. I sat the 11+ and thankfully passed. Then there was a trip to the Co-op on Westoe Road to be kitted out in my new uniform. I loved my new blazer & pinafore and could not wait to wear it.
When I started the South Shields Grammar School in Sept.1970 the Lower School was based at the Mowbray Annexe; Mrs Burns as Head. The Upper School was based on Iolanthe Terrace with Miss Gillian Harris as overall Head although for day to day concerns we were answerable to Mrs Burns. Although based at the lower school we did have some lessons on Iolanthe Terrace. This used to be quite a highlight because Westoe Boys' School was right next door. I remember having my lovely regulation school scarf pinched by one of the boys! However any contact with the boys was really frowned on.
I remember life at the old Grammar School to be very strict & the old buildings (& some of the teachers— Miss Brewis was still there) just seemed to echo discipline. There were very few brave enough not to toe the line. That said, I actually enjoyed school and loved to fill my 'Woolies' briefcase with endless amounts of homework and projects. My new best friend encouraged me to join Westoe Tennis Club and we used to have some great times together.
If we were to take a second language we were streamed accordingly into classes 1'O', 1'P', 1'Q'; I was in 1'O' & attempted to learn Russian as well as French!! The non-

language classes were 1'R' and 1'S' & the added class when we got to third year was class 1'T' which comprised the last girls to take the 13+.

In September 1972 the school moved to brand new premises & became known as the King George Comp. for Girls. There was an amazing change in the attitude of pupils & the difference between old school & new school could not have been more stark. The new school felt more like a hospital with everything bright and clinical but it seemed that the old draconian type of discipline had been left behind at the old school.(of course some of us remained goody-two-shoes throughout)!!'

School life moved on, friendships were made and boy friends fought over. However in our 4th year we had to face the tragic loss of our much loved friend, Katie Boyes. Katie was popular with everybody, full of fun, never ever down. She had a close family – loved life – loved Rod Stewart. I feel very lucky to have had Katie as a friend.

Spring'74: L.to R. Wendy Dawson, Alison Gray, Katie Boyes, Ashley Turnbull – Janet at the front.

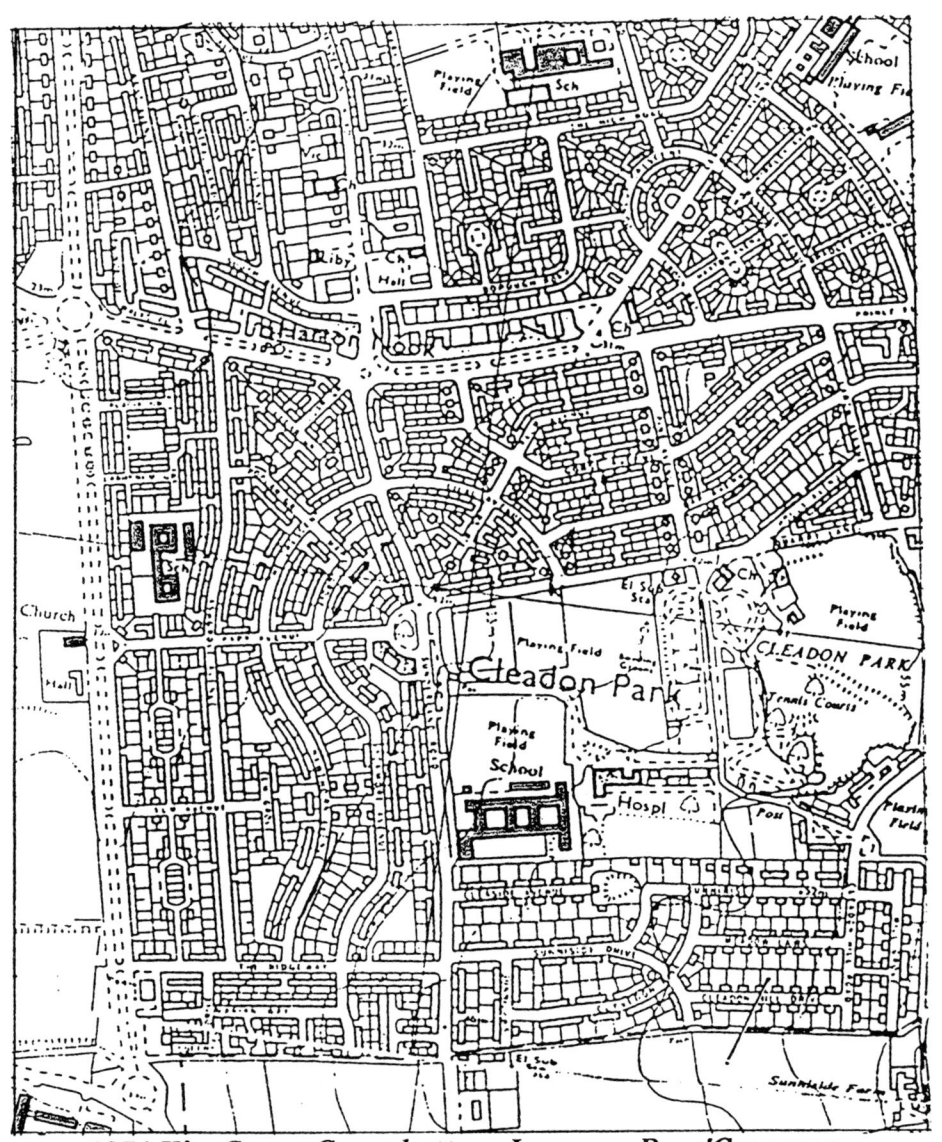

*1974:KingGeorgeComp.bottom L corner.Boys'Grammar top centre built 1936. Cleadon Park I.&J.built 1926/30 (Ridgeway).Cleadon Park Seniors'1938.Harton I&J 1938 top R.corner.Redwell built 1952 just off map on R.*

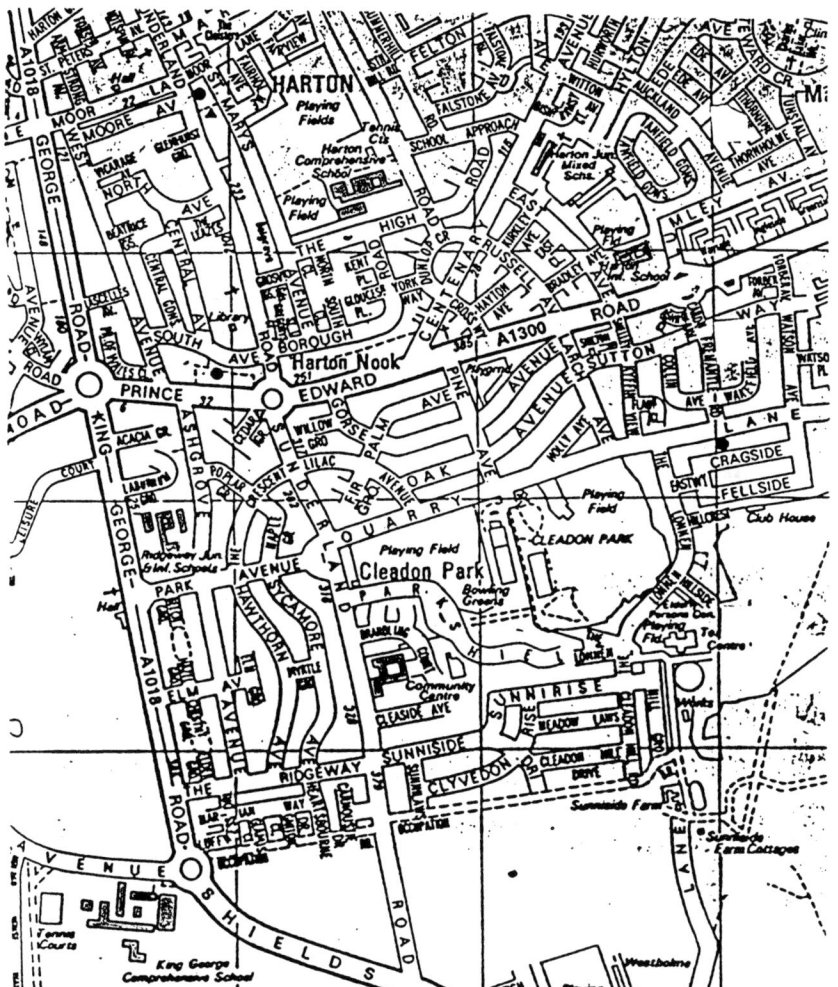

*1988:KingGeorgeComp.bottomL.corner.Boys' Grammar now Harton Comp. Harton J.&I.mixed. Redwell Comp. just off on R. Ridgeway J.&I.mixed,(wasCleadon Park) NO Cleadon Park Comp. (part of it on Sunderland Rd. now a Community Centre.)* It is interesting to compare (p42/3)the style of Harton Grammar 1936,Cleadon Park 1938. Falling-rolls & reorganisation probably brought about the demise of Cleadon Park Seniors.

*1970s continued*         *Janet Erickson*

'Gone were the freezing cold outside loos & the occasional crunch of cockroach underfoot, but we missed the lovely old fashioned chemistry labs and the characterless breeze block replacements were less than inspiring. Looking back I'm really pleased I had those first two years at the proper old Grammar School.
My good friend Ashley Wood (we went through High School together) went on to university, then teacher training. She returned to South Shields just as the King George Comp.for Girls and Harton Comp. for Boys were going mixed.(Sept.1980) She did part of her training at Cleadon Park Seniors' just before it closed & recalls the great upheaval at that time when existing teachers at the separate boy/girl comprehensives had to apply for their own jobs. I do not think anybody could have been more aware of the changes that took place from 1970 to 1980 than Ashley – having started that decade as a pupil under the traditional Grammar School system and ended the decade as a teacher under the new mixed Comprehensive School system.'

I feel Janet's writing gives some real insight into the 70s & points of interest:the mention of Gilbert St. built 1908: the discussion (p78) that the Girls' High School would be mixed and in fact remained single sex until 1980; that Miss Harris maintained discipline in the old system but there was a 'different' discipline in the new.

The word 'upheaval' & the fact that Ashley did her teaching practice in a school about to close, sheds some light on the following piece of writing. My nephew wrote a vivid account of his last years at school – his chance to let off steam! But it does show how radical changes affect both pupils & teachers caught in that change & disrupts established patterns for good or ill.

*Cleadon Park Seniors'    Courtesy of Graham Erickson*
I can still remember in perfect detail, the layout of the school. It seemed huge at the time. Whilst it is not there now to check I am sure it was probably quite small. I am obsessed at the shift of scale through memory. Maybe I will go to the town hall & try to see plans to confirm this.

I am always astonished when I see schools now: teachers wearing soft, leisure clothing & laughing with pupils. Different from scowling figures in ancient black suits, cutting the air with trusty canes, warning for anyone who might just do anything. The school, like many of those who taught there, was of course on its last legs; due to close. (1980) There were some teachers who projected consideration and intelligence but in my memory they were few and far between.

We boys were educated to work in industry... I voiced a desire to go to Art College. I was disappointed that teachers derided this. I was upset when my Dad similarly criticised it.

I also remember feeling domestically privileged. Whilst, as a family, we never went without anything we weren't wealthy by any stretch of the imagination. Here, there were kids near ragged, deprived – I hope to God I never gloated – & other pupils who provided friendship as strong as any I have ever known. I always felt proud when my friends came to my home.

To my shame I joined in with the mob... I jettisoned my young intellect to ensure a physically easy ride. I learned that dumbing down avoided the glare of attention. I am tempted to amend my recollections and invent a set of happy school memories...

At the outset of writing this I had hundreds of hateful visions of school jumping around. I was going to say that if you excavated the grounds of the school you would find the remains of hope, ambition and dreams. Thinking about it now I think I just didn't like school!

*Above: Harton Nursery School 1967. Graham aged 3, dark jumper & little smile, centre front. Below, Harton Juniors. 1969. Janet, extreme L. with school friends.*

*Harton Infants 1967 School 1967-1970*

*Mandy, extreme right, 2nd row from the front.*

*Courtesy of Mandy Erickson*

Dear Aunty Mary...

I started school life in 1967 at Harton Infants'. My teacher, Mrs Gordon had a pet rat in the classroom & frequently it sat on her shoulder. It sounds strange now but it was taken very naturally back then. She was a really nice teacher. I then went to Harton Juniors' in '69-73. My next strong memory is of the time I was sitting in my little school chair, backwards, weaving my legs in and out of the wooden lats until I got so stuck I had to be led bent double to the caretaker's office to be sawn free. My early memories are sketchy and few. My next memory of my last year in Junior school, was awful thoughts of the 11plus looming. I was absolutely dreading it, knowing I was going to fail miserably. I remember the day clearly. The Head Teacher came into the classroom very solemnly and announced the 'sad' news that the 11plus had been cancelled from that year so our class was the first year not to sit. The class was silent except for one person who let out an obviously joyful gasp, amid the groans & disappointed faces. I was so happy I could have jumped up & down!

I was then sent to Cleadon Park Comp.'73-79. I liked the first couple of years. It was so different at big school, more exciting. It was fun sussing out the teachers; which ones we could get away with what, some were so laid back, some were almost afraid, but some you just did not mess with, really, really strict. I saw some awful things, some really funny things, some sad things. I didn't think it at the time, but infant and junior school just didn't prepare you for your time in a rough senior school. I hope you find this helpful.

## *The Ninth Decade*                    *1980 to 1989*

For this decade, I have not sought out any 'young' voices. Nor have I searched through cuttings or lists for solid facts.

Two reasons: By the time we reach an age of interest in our roots, people who hold the answers are no longer around! I feel I have caught something of the earlier decades *just in time*. There isn't such an urgency for the 80s & 90s. They are within reach of the next 'one' to record this history of schools. Also I want to pay some attention to the children of today; they too are an important part of the history of this century.

Suffice to say that the minutes of the Education Committee show a continuation of matters great and small in the management of South Shields schools.

In the fifties, new schools were needed because of the 'bulge'. In the seventies and eighties old schools met their demise because of reorganisation, 'falling-rolls' & housing development.

Nursery education was the next priority: units were

attached to existing schools & new nursery schools were built. At first provision was patchy, concentration was in 'priority' areas but by the end of the eighties most young children could expect a nursery place.
That great edifice, Westoe Schools, was pulled down in the late 80s (including 'my' Girls' High School on Iolanthe Terrace). Left standing was Westoe Infants' & a new Nursery was built on the site beside the school. Old schools still had there uses. Cone Street had been used as factory premises before demolition in 1956, but more importantly some were used for 'further education.' Ocean Road was for a time a community centre. In the mid 80s part of Stanhope Complex became the West Park Community Assoc. Its role was flexible and housed all manner of further education. It catered for every age; for groups of varied interests; it met needs for mothers/toddlers, ethnic groups & provided respite for carers. Subjects ranged from writing to keep fit!
In the early 90s, *Write Together* was able to use one of the classrooms as an office cum writing room. It had high windows, good wood floors, big old radiators & was very comfortable. New schools have shorter lives; in 1990 Redwell School came down.(1952-1990) Educ. minutes show a continuum of decisions large & small: from sinks to building alterations, from school dinner supervision to size of classes, implementation of government record-keeping to curriculum & staffing.

*The Tenth Decade*                     *1990 to 1999*
*Schools and Children of the Nineties*
I started this study with a number of questions in mind: Which was my mother's school & how could I confirm my early memories of Cleadon Park Infants? My mother was born in 1900 & I believe she went to Westoe. Consequently I followed the history of Westoe Schools fairly closely. For myself born in 1930, I tried

to record accurate facts about Cleadon Park Infants & Junior school. Once again, a change of title – now it is: 'Ridgeway County Junior&Mixed Infants' as from 1975. Throughout this study I worked to a tight framework; 96pages in all, so many pages for each decade, & invariably I overran. The 1980s barely appear, because I wanted the last decade to feature today's children & with difficulty I kept exactly eight pages clear.

I approached both Ridgeway & Westoe Schools and asked if I could photograph the pupils and the school buildings. As it turned out I arranged to visit Westoe Infants' in time for morning playtime; my visit to Ridgeway JMI was for early afternoon and I'd made a request to the Head to see my old classroom.

Perhaps I should have visited a Comprehensive school to end this study, having covered the great debates which preceded this historical change in education. Even today the debate continues, not just in South Shields but nationwide.

I prefer to concentrate on the very young; they will grow up in the next Millennium. Hopefully, the tried & true infant and junior schools offer children the right environment for good education.

The debate over methods in comprehensive schools goes on. Studies state that exam results show no difference whether cross-setting or mixed ability teaching is used. (NFER Telegraph Dec.1998) Some research shows that by seating boys & girls alternately in class, the girls continued to work hard and boys were less distracted by other boys and concentrated more. This search to perfect schools for senior pupils seems inevitable. The need for the above studies indicate, some boys are less motivated to learn & under-achieve; streaming could result in low self-esteem & truancy. This age of puberty seems to grow more difficult to manage year by year. Comprehensive schools are large, in order to offer a wide range of subjects. The two facts together; large schools and adolescent pupils, require almost superhuman management. Gone are the smaller manageable schools where a good head knew every teacher, knew every pupil, and more importantly, each pupil felt noticed.

I repeat what I said earlier; children bring their fears to school. I think I need to add to that now; many TV fed youngsters today, also bring their rebellions. The need to balance all these factors & still offer good education is the reason why policies are always under review.

*Photo:Ridgeway J.&M.I 1998      Head: Mr B. Winter (Change of title 1975: Cleadon Park to Ridgeway)*

*Ridgeway School is just as I remember it when I went there in 1935 to 1941. It is in a typical thirties style. (Cragside, Newcastle is very similar) The two wooden buildings of my infant school are gone now. Inside, the open verandahs around the quadrangles are closed in.*

*Visit to Ridgeway JMI.1.12.1998   Head:Mr B Winter.
Top Juniors; 10/11 years of age, tables pulled together, busily working on a 1998 Christmas display. I asked to see this room. In 1940/41 at this same age, in this same room I spent two scholarship years with Miss Bailey. I sat centre back; girls' desks one side, boys' the other.*
It was a miserable day when I visited Ridgeway school. I'd walked along Ashgrove: no privet hedges now and on such a day the gardens looked depressing. But my old home had a new front door & 'my' pillar box, which on a previous visit had been daubed in black & silver paint, was again a healthy red.
Inside the school, I was made welcome: after taking photographs outside I was able to take 'snaps' of the pupils in their classrooms. The school secretary was my guide – little did she know how nostalgic I felt.

*The colour & busy, happy six year olds all at work so struck me that I took this snap & then asked 'May I?' How can a photograph capture the good atmosphere; the smiling teacher & her industrious class.*

A Walk Back in Time!

A brass plaque in the junior hall shows *This School opened 24th April 1931.* The newspaper cutting about the event answered many of my early questions. The long wooden school I remembered was converted from the Cleadon Park Estate site office & store. A further classroom was built nearby for £250. (Educ.Minutes) In all six classes.(350 pupils) This same cutting described the 'semi-detached' school with infant/junior halls & quadrangles. As to changes:I saw tables instead of rows of desks; a 'technical aids' room, a class in the library all reading until I disturbed them! A room filled with books would have been a wonderland in the 30s.

Some history comes back to me. In 1939 the Junior Hall was used as a branch library until a new one was built after the war beside the old Palladium. Once a week, we chose a book to take home from the children's section. I still remember those first books. Perhaps those few books were the basis of today's school library.

I was given a 'history' of Ridgeway School – I am still finding tiny details of huge interest to me. My early teachers are named & Miss Bailey is *'Gladys'*. Amazing! Also 5 classrooms to accomodate 250 children!!

*The Infants' Hall. At once, I had a clear flashback of 1935: Prayers, Miss Henderson on the low dais, me at five feeling guilty because 'far too many milk straws are used.' Of course I wanted a photograph. A Nativity frieze was 'in progress' & eight of today's children sat along the edge of that long remembered platform.*

I felt I travelled a long way back that afternoon – & the school, so many classrooms, so many children, a great responsibility. I was reminded of a remark by an older teacher:'In the thirties, a class of 48 was far easier than a present day class of 30.' but in class after class, smiling faces, navy blue tops & a good atmosphere. Teaching is not a soft option & I was very impressed.

*Westoe County Infants' School     Head: Mrs L.Lilico*
*Visit: 17.11.1998*
In my letter to Mrs Lilico I explained I'd followed the history of Westoe Schools & was it possible to take a 'snap' of the school & hopefully of the children too.
It just seemed right to end the 20th century not only with children of the nineties but with this Victorian school built in 1891!

*The Visit 17.11.1998*　　　　*Westoe Infants' School*
It was a bright cold day as I walked up the bank to the school. The same bank I'd walked up so many times in 1941 to the High School on Iolanthe Terrace. I stopped on the corner of St.Michaels'Terrace. Westoe Infants' School was in full sun and I took my first 'snap'.
As I stepped into the school I glimpsed children in classrooms but the hall was empty. I met Mrs Lilico & she showed me a box of school memorabilia. The school had celebrated its century: 1891-1991. There were photographs of the event, of the children & a fine history of the school. The morning Assembly was at ten past ten. There was a small chair in the hall for me with permission to take photographs. MrsL.spoke from the centre & children filed in from either end. Soon the hall was a sea of blue jumpers & everyone sitting cross legged. I was delighted. This was just what I wanted.

*Westoe Infants'. Children in the school-yard. 17.11.1998*
In Assembly, one girl had a Blue Peter award & it was shown to the the children, then 'Hands together' & a short prayer. Christmas hadn't started but the children sang their first carol; *Away in a Manger*. I caught a timeless feeling, quiet and reassuring.

I joined the children at play time and the change of colour was amazing. In place of the blue tops, the yard was filled with coats & hats of every hue – the clothes of the late 90s, a piece of history in itself. The ground was a little slippery and the children were warned. At this age, children play well – I saw no tears or play fights. I watched ring games & clapping games and was asked to take photos but not pestered. I don't think the children were on their best behaviour, they were too busy playing. The 'snaps' caught some lovely moments.

*17.11.1998 Westoe Infants at playtime, all smiles.*
At the bell, the children stood still and I was able to take this snap. Back inside groups of children were investigating 'Light' with one child recording. Mrs Lilico gave me some idea of Curriculum & Early Science but she did say that it had been improved; was less complex. She said there were nine classes, 220 pupils & added that there was *talk of a new school ahead.*

I enjoyed both visits and if smiles and friendly children are anything to go by I feel very heartened as those children move into the next millennium.

Throughout I've asked questions & offered opinions. In South Shields I was given a very good education as were many many others. On my recent visits I took my pride to Ridgeway School & I wasn't disappointed. And Westoe School: I feel I've caught just a little of its history *just in time.* More than that; I wonder if my mother Lily May, once played in that same schoolyard, many, many years ago? I like to think she did.